PRAISE
THE GRATITUDE BLUEPRINT:

"This is a must read for anyone ready to make the switch from mild or chronic anxiety to true happiness becoming your new set point! This book makes what seems insurmountable so easy. The simple yet precise practices can legitimately transform your life into a thriving one ... so much so that you will want to buy copies for all of your friends and family. It is that kind of book—a book that heals lives!"

—VERONICA KRESTOW, MA, author of *The Diamond Process* and cofounder of the Diamond Process Coach Training Program

"This is no ordinary book you hold in your hands as FMTG is no ordinary toolkit. It is a divination! When I started reading, every word spoke to my heart and the fibers of my being. I had always thought I was a grateful person but doing FMTG daily made me realize that I used gratitude as a passing, momentary thought. It was not a habit, so it had never truly replaced my other thoughts in a proactive manner. As I continued to practice, I was awed at the peace, harmony, and positive outlook I started having—a healing process was going on. The excitement of creating the blueprint of my life with gratitude has been powerful for me."

—SWATI TANEJA (Canada)

"I was blessed to be included in the original gratitude experiment Waleuska Lazo ran on Facebook, in which she generously shared her personal process for overcoming pain and illness. The experience was life changing for me because it showed me I wasn't fully acknowledging the good things in my life. I was on autopilot. Waleuska's system helped me to grab the wheel of my life and live deliberately and gratefully. Thanks to her, I will never let go again."

—BARRY MCCARTHY (United States)

"If you want to let go of what does not serve you and manifest the life you've always dreamed of having, *The Gratitude Blueprint* is the book you must read. With this daily practice, I've shifted gears and hit new heights of mindfulness. I've changed my relationships with myself and with others. The quality of my thankfulness is more heartfelt. I look at everything and everyone now with genuine appreciation and love. It all begins with the heart."

—NISH TAKIA (India)

"In *The Gratitude Blueprint*, Waleuska Lazo teaches a nurturing, step-by-step process. Her FMTG method is a gracious, deeply transformative program that involves so much more than learning how to excel in giving gratitude. Without doubt, it is one of the safest, gentlest, yet most liberating processes I've done on my road of self-transformation. The key to the success of this formula for me was that I could do it in the privacy of my home and take myself easily to the places I needed to heal. I learned how to both forgive past issues and celebrate life. This was the first system I've used where I could connect my heart and mind as I visualized. I cannot recommend this book highly enough."

—ELIZABETH DWYER (Austria)

"I am profoundly grateful to have discovered the teachings of Waleuska Lazo. I lost my spiritual teacher a few years back and was searching for something that resonated, and FMTG has been the answer I sought. My five-minute meditation in the morning helps set a positive start to the day. It helps me slow down, pay attention to my surroundings, and focus on everything that is going right in my life. I've learned that by truly focusing on the positive, I create more of it."

—TERRY BERGDOLL (United States)

"*The Gratitude Blueprint* taught me how to shine a spotlight on my dark and hidden places of fear in regards to relationships. Because of unspeakable abuse in two consecutive marriages, followed by a brutal rape and a diagnosis of cancer, I was completely shut off from romantic love even though I have always said I wanted to experience a real marriage. Gradually, I used FMTG to address the areas that needed healing, finding some tiny thing to be grateful for in each, and slowly my emotions and feelings began to shift. I was alone for eleven years, then Waleuska encouraged me to draw up a comprehensive blueprint covering every area of my life, including finding the 'perfect husband.' Finally, I was ready. I committed it to the Lord and let it go. Two months after releasing the blueprint, I 'saw'

Ben. To make a long story short, he proposed a short while later and I accepted. Every moment together is pure joy, and I am so incredibly grateful to Waleuska for her encouragement and assistance in taking me from the expectancy of spending the rest of my life alone to being a happily married and cherished wife."

—MAUREEN SULLIVAN (South Africa)

"The FMTG program is spectacular. Each week is as incredible as the prior week and together the weeks build more and more into touching upon all the many facets of life we should be grateful for, including so much that we easily take for granted! Another thing I find amazing is that this program is all encompassing and has superbly organized the most important aspects of a higher, healthier level of being! It truly is a complete package because the final week gives you clear directions on how to create the life of your dreams! First it teaches you to be grateful for having a life, then it teaches you how to make your life more amazing! The lesson of the final day of *The Gratitude Blueprint* is such an incredibly brilliant way to sum it up, carry it with us, and live it every single day."

—JOHN ARTINIAN (United States)

"I was drawn to the FMTG system immediately. I love that this technique is proven to support emotional and physical healing. It inspires me that Waleuska found purpose in her pain and chose to share her knowledge. Her passion and compassion are second to none. I have gone through the program four times and counting, continuing to learn ways to heal and find my most authentic self each time. Every topic in the twenty-eight-day program is thought provoking."

—JULIE KESSLER (United States)

"Words cannot describe how valuable doing twenty-eight days of gratitude has been to me. At first, I was anxious thinking I would be hard pressed to find the time. Little did I know that FMTG would completely take over my life. I eagerly turned five minutes into 40,320 minutes and immersed myself in the best, most beautiful experience. So much so I have signed up to repeat the next course so the joy I've learned to develop can deepen. Try it, you'll love it. You certainly won't regret it!"

—JENNY SMITH (England)

"My gratitude for life has grown exponentially due to this program. I'm at the beginning of a new life—and not just a new chapter in life, a new book. A completely rewritten life. *The Gratitude Blueprint* and its FMTG technique has reawakened my heart and mind, stirring in me a discontent for the old and teaching me what a life of gratitude really means. I will be forever grateful for Waleuska's guidance."

—LARA MARIE FORD (United States)

"The year 2020 shook the world with the jolt of COVID-19. However, there were many who experienced an upgrade in their personal lives. I was amongst them. January 20, 2020, was the date when I took up FMTG for the first time. And then there was no looking back. Four times in a row I enrolled myself for this beautifully crafted practice of gratitude by Waleuska. Not that I had gone through some devastating life situation earlier, but I had also not encountered the inner hidden jewel of the art of living life more meaningfully, mindfully, and extremely joyfully. FMTG fashioned my subconscious into a positive magic box and all I can think of now is gratitude and more gratitude in each passing moment of my life, thereby enriching and enhancing the beautiful encounter with the thing called life. And for this, I remain immensely and eternally grateful to Waleuska and her wonderful program called FMTG."

—DR. MITA SHARMA (Indonesia)

"Twenty-eight days of personal investment and development spent cocooned in a supportive, nurturing family of fellow fans bonded by a common love of living life to the full. Content, pace, delivery—all get five stars. I highly recommend FMTG as a global human entitlement. Everyone deserves this experience. Everyone! Namaste and thank you."

—DEBBIE PERCY (United Kingdom)

THE GRATITUDE BLUEPRINT

THE ULTIMATE STRATEGY FOR EXTRAORDINARY HAPPINESS

WALEUSKA LAZO

DREAMCATCHER PRINT

DreamCatcher Print / Waleuska Lazo
www.waleuskalazo.com

Copy editing and book production by Stephanie Gunning
Cover design by Gus Yoo

Special discounts are available on quantity purchases by corporations and associations. For details, contact the publisher.

Library of Congress Control Number 2021902426

The Gratitude Blueprint / Waleuska Lazo —1st ed.

ISBN 978-1-7327431-5-1 (paperback)

DEDICATION

To the amazing group of Gratituders who took part in the original Gratitude Experiment Course, FMTG. In generously helping me test the concepts and strategies of this book, you took the Gratitude Blueprint to the next level.

We began as strangers from different parts of the world. We ended as friends who, in a very short time, knew each other to the depths of our souls. Despite having different challenges to overcome and fears to face, we united with a common purpose to use the power of gratitude to transform our lives.

CONTENTS

PREFACE

THE MOTHER OF ALL VIRTUES IS GRATITUDE.

B efore we embark on this journey together, let me express my gratitude to you for connecting with me through these pages and for your willingness to embrace the powerful habit of gratitude during the next four weeks.

This book is about how you can learn to live a grateful life—and everything that follows from it. Plain and simple. This practice isn't associated with any religious doctrine. It isn't science-based but incorporates scientific principles that have been proven. It is about the special gifts of gratitude that an ordinary woman discovered for herself in a time of physical and emotional need.

For a long time, I kept the method I'm about to share with you to myself. What began as a simple exercise I did upon waking and before getting out of bed first thing in the morning in a desperate attempt to turn the facts of my existence around—in an effort to heal my body, mind, and spirit—was so powerfully transformative that very soon I began to reap the rewards. At first, I was unaware of the changes taking place in my life. Things began to happen so organically and unexpectedly that I did not immediately connect the dots. In fact, I was oblivious to the ways my personality and energy were changing until those around me began to comment. Then I realized I had stumbled upon something magical, a state of being that is the precursor for lasting happiness.

For you to believe my promise that the habit I'm advocating works as well as it does, I feel it's important to give you a clear picture of the person I was prior to my discovery. Frankly, I was a controlling, type A, relentlessly bitchy, and unhappy person. Ouch, it hurts me to admit that I was so rough on the people around me back then, but that's the honest truth. I held people to high, often unrealistic standards and pressured them to accede to my demands. I was especially hard on myself. I was never satisfied. No matter what anyone did to please me, including me, it was never enough.

In my professional career as the cofounder, with my husband at that time, of a successful startup company, which for many years was my focus in life, my employees took the brunt of my ill temper. If I was having a bad day, everyone around me paid the price. Although the business was financially successful, sustained the hundreds of people we employed, and made a positive impact in the communities it served, I never felt satisfied.

I paid attention to the stressful aspects of running the business, speaking rudely to my workers, and complaining about the hardships we encountered. I griped about our competitors rather than praising our team for their persistence and loyalty. The list of things I blamed for my dissatisfaction was long.

Reality was different from how I felt about it. I was unimpressed that in spite of limited resources, our company was one of the most successful in the industry. Because of my negative mindset, I missed out on the joy and fun of accomplishment and the magic of my collaboration with my husband. We had started out working side by side to change the social fabric of society. Our shared vision carried us through many highs and lows. Before our nine-figure exit, we had built an eLearning business that had over a million enrollments worldwide. Still, I was dissatisfied.

Sadly, I lived in a state of lack for over twenty years—always scheming, wishing, and lamenting. I took everything I had for granted. *Everything!* Despite many blessings, including that of being the mother of two beautiful daughters, I mainly focused on the things I didn't have that I thought I needed to feel good about myself.

Talk about feeling ungrateful, huh?

I regret that I wasted as much time as I did focusing on the negative, when I could have chosen to celebrate the ingenuity, creativity, passion, and commitment that our people brought to work each day. I could have rejoiced at the foresight of my business partners, which put us ahead of the curve. What my husband and I had built, along with our business partner, was nothing short of a miracle for two kids right out of university, who initially worked out of their bedroom with one computer and a modem.

In my personal life, I behaved even worse than I did at the office. Instead of focusing on the goodness of being married to a man who was loyal, saw the best in me, appreciated my qualities, and celebrated my every accomplishment, I chose to focus on the lack of time he had for me. Rather than seeing the good in him, I craved adventure. I thought I was missing out.

Hindsight is 20/20. I now can see that I was already on the biggest adventure of my lifetime.

Although I may have been unkind to my husband, I treated myself worse. I was never satisfied with who I was. I never felt like I was loved enough. I expended a lot of energy on disliking myself and trying to be someone else. I survived for about twenty years on a strict diet of "rabbit food" — salads and egg whites—never truly enjoying eating the foods I liked. And all for what? To satisfy an obsession with reaching a certain weight. I was driven to hit a certain number on the scale, a cause to which I was enslaved daily. Any time I missed this goal, I became unhappy. It would strip away my self-confidence and esteem. I was always striving for an ideal of perfection that was unattainable at best and destructive at worst. Yet, I could have chosen to be grateful for the figure I already had. I could have chosen to be grateful that I was healthy. During that dark period in my life, none of the beautiful things in my life registered.

The struggle of always trying to attain a physical standard that I believed I had not achieved made me feel deprived and probably contributed to me becoming someone who wasn't happy. I was enveloped in the love of my daughters, husband, and friends, yet I had no gratitude for their presence. Looking back now, I see I was like a plug pulled from an electric socket and was disconnected from my soul. My existence was shallow and empty.

The one thing I knew was that I felt unhappy. But rather than looking within and making changes there that would bring me contentment and peace, I blamed external things for my dissatisfaction.

Where did all this lead? To worse eating habits, sickness, body dysmorphia, and divorce, and afterward, into a toxic relationship that further eroded my already low self-esteem and left me heartbroken after it ended.

When I hit my version of rock bottom, when my body got so sick I could no longer function, I decided to try something I had not tried before. That "something" was cultivating the habit of gratitude in my daily life.

One afternoon, the pain of my emotions was so unbearable that it brought me to my knees with tears pouring down my face. I stayed in that painful state, lying on my cold bathroom floor, in silence. It's amazing what you can hear if you stay still long enough. I still remember the magical moment like it was yesterday. I heard a knock on my soul's door, and that was the day I choose to birth myself anew. The next morning, lying in my bed, I began to count my blessings. This simple action forever changed the trajectory of my life.

That act of counting my blessings gave life to the system I will be sharing with you in this book.

Today, after walking a spiritual path for half a decade, I am well and happy. I feel at ease in my skin. People who hear my story often ask what I did to get out the emotional hole I had dug myself into, and I tell them that there is no big secret. They can do it as easily as I did—once they are ready. As with anything else that's worthwhile, my turnaround took diligent, consistent work. I needed to become aware of my unconscious thoughts, emotions, and unconscious behavior patterns. Once I began to look at myself objectively from the inside out, transforming my life was sometimes like taking three steps forward and two back and having the discipline, drive, and self-love to stay committed to the path—that's how I transformed my life.

I have been fortunate to study with amazing teachers. Inspired by their example, I have adopted a few simple habits that I continue to practice on a consistent basis. These daily habits have enabled me to experience a happier and more peaceful life. Among these habits, cultivating gratitude is the one that stands out as the single most important to embrace.

Welcoming gratitude is a simple habit that takes only five minutes first thing in the morning. The magic of my system is not in the five minutes but in the cumulative effect those five minutes each day of your life produces.

If there was one thing and one thing only that you could do that would be crucial to your personal evolution, fulfillment, and wellbeing, gratitude is the one I recommend. I can tell you this with so much certainty because I am a living testament to the power of gratitude to make us whole.

In this book, you will hear me say that gratitude is the precursor to happiness. You will hear me say this repeatedly both because I believe it and because I want you always to remember it. When you learn to evoke the feeling of gratitude, you ignite a force inside you that becomes more powerful than any fear, doubt, and guilt you feel or hardships that stand against you. You possess, within you, the blueprint to live a healthy and grateful life. But a blueprint without a contractor simply remains a simple blueprint and nothing else. It needs a contractor to make it into what is meant to become, such as a house, a building, or a skyscraper. The same is true of your blueprint. You are the contractor and master of your own fate. You will learn that your thoughts, emotions, and behavior are what signals and ignites your gratitude blueprint to activate. Once activated, you will experience a love, peace, and zest for life that will cascade into all areas of your life, including your health.

What differentiates successful people from unsuccessful people are their habits. From the single habit of gratitude, I have healed my body, mind, and spirit, become a nicer person—a woman people want to be around—and altered my negative programming. I love the person I am becoming day by day, and I enjoy watching myself evolve. I enjoy excellent, authentic relationships with people I value. My work is meaningful and uplifting and makes a positive impact on people's lives. I feel that I am at last living the life I was meant to live. Most importantly, I feel joyful and at peace.

Although it took me longer to register the full immensity of the transformation that would result from my new gratitude habit, I had already experienced such positive results within the first four weeks that I could see that my efforts, such as they were, had been rewarded. Once my gratitude blueprint was kindled, a fire in my soul was ignited, and the Universe began to conspire with me to give me additional knowledge that allowed me to remake myself and enjoy a state of unwavering happiness.

When I embarked on writing this book, I wanted to test the concepts that had worked for me on a group of strangers. On Facebook, I asked for twenty volunteers to go through a four-week online experience I created. I called it the Gratitude Experiment because that is what it was, an experiment. I didn't achieve my goal of twenty people. Instead, and to my pleasant surprise, nearly 250 people volunteered, and I chose thirty-five. I asked them to complete a short questionnaire before and after completing the experiment. Participants were of both genders and were between thirty and seventy years of age. I purposely chose a combination of people who were familiar with giving gratitude and those who were not. Some people reported feeling satisfied with their lives, some were semi-satisfied, and some were at a low point in their lives.

The results were amazing! Except for one person, all participants reported higher levels in their overall life satisfaction at the end compared to where they were at the beginning. In other words, 97 percent of the participants walked away from the Gratitude Experiment feeling more satisfied and happier with their lives than before they started. The one person whose life satisfaction did not change asked to reenroll in the course. Even though his quality of life had not yet changed, he saw the value of the practice and wished to pursue it. All the participants reported having higher knowledge of what gratitude truly is and how to apply it in their daily lives. One woman said, "You opened so many different facets of gratitude for me that I realize now how little I knew." Another participant said, "It is amazing how gratitude has changed my perspective of life in a matter of a few weeks. Morning gratitude has become my 'first cup of coffee' for the day."

Questions were scored on a scale from one to ten. An interesting part was that people who originally reported scoring a nine or ten for their knowledge and familiarity with gratitude adjusted their original numbers at the end of the course. These people shared that there was more to gratitude than is commonly understood, or at least was more than they had previously considered. Another participant said, "Through this practice, you have shown me to show up in my own life. I learned how essential it is to carve out enough time for myself to spend time with me, to show myself the love and care that I deserve and need and then to share that with others."

If you'd like to be happy and reshape an aspect of your life—anything at all—like I did, the five minutes of gratitude habit described in this book is the key. I promise that if you try this system, as prescribed, on a consistent, daily basis for the next twenty-eight days, your mindset and moods will improve. You will feel more energized and less irritable or anxious. Your relationships and health can improve. You may be surprised at how quickly everything changes for the better—from the smallest of things to the most major. You may even begin to experience synchronicities and miracles in your life.

INTRODUCTION

THE GRATITUDE BLUEPRINT

BE MINDFUL OF YOUR THOUGHTS, FOR YOU GIVE LIFE TO EVERYTHING YOU THINK OR SAY ALOUD.

Learning to live with a perpetual attitude of gratitude changed my life. For this reason, I advise everyone I meet to start each day in a state of gratitude.

Recently, I had an epiphany. Although everyone has an idea of what gratitude is, not everyone knows *how* to practice being grateful to the point it becomes automatic, second nature, like breathing. I've called the Introduction "The Gratitude Blueprint" because that is what I wish for you to understand. You already have this blueprint within you. It is part of your DNA, and if you practice igniting it, you will end up with a full heart and a life filled with a richness of connection, meaning, health, and beauty. Your life can be a beautiful experiment in ever-increasing gratefulness.

Before we start, there are a few important things you need to know. First, let's demystify the popular belief that gratitude comes easier to those with greater financial means. Many believe, *Affluent people feel more grateful because they have more reasons to be thankful.*

Not true, except on the surface. I've been on both sides of the fence and can say with certainty that money can buy many things except happiness.

Wealth or poverty has nothing to do with our ability to feel gratitude. Being grateful is a subjective experience that is not dependent on our outer circumstances.

Some people believe, *Happiness or contentment leads to gratitude.* But it's the other way around. Grateful people feel happier than ungrateful people.

There are many people who appear to have everything but are unhappy and ungrateful. (I should know, I used to be one of them!) There are also people who are no strangers to adversity and misfortune who are deeply grateful and happy. (I also should know, as I'm now one of them!)

The word *gratitude* means different things to different people. But it is commonly believed that gratitude is the appreciation we feel when something good has happened for us or someone we love, or that it is the emotion we feel in the presence of something pleasing.

This is where I have an issue with popular beliefs. If gratitude is conditional, then wouldn't this mean that we should only feel gratitude for positive things and events?

My contention is—no—that real gratitude is so much more. In fact, finding things to be grateful for in negative events, both during and after they were occurring, has possibly transformed me the most dramatically of anything I have actively contemplated.

So, what is gratitude?

For me, gratitude is the experience of feeling fulfilled, at peace, and content with all that you already have in its totality. I say *in its totality* because that is the key. It means you are at peace with all that you once had and currently have. You feel at peace and accepting of your sorrows, troubles, losses, regrets, and grief, as well as of your blessings. It means being able to cast aside judgment when you're in a difficult situation and appreciate that you were selected to undergo the experience for a purpose—even if you don't know what the purpose or reason is at present. It means accepting that you may never know the reasons why.

In the last five years, I've learned that being able to look at everything in your life—the good and the not so good— and honestly say, "I am grateful for it all. I may not have deserved what I've been through, but I am appreciative of the lessons." Even amid pain, finding something to be grateful for is incredibly powerful. It makes you resilient. When you can love your life to that extent, eliciting emotions of gratefulness for it all, you become unstoppable.

We also must be realistic. Getting to this point doesn't happen overnight. It requires patience and a commitment to look at life through a set of thankful lenses *regardless* of the circumstances.

How do you live the life you're destined to live? *By practicing gratitude.*

Rewiring Your Brain for Gratitude

When you learn something new, as you are doing right now, your brain cells begin firing and creating new neurological connections. Unless you repeat the same thoughts and behaviors on a daily basis, those new connections wither away in days and never penetrate into the medial sections of the brain where your subconscious mind resides.[1] But when you continue to practice what you are learning, pathways—whole networks—of thought and ability are built, reinforced, and strengthened.

Five Minutes to Gratitude® (FMTG) is a simple, step-by-step system that helps you "hardwire" your subconscious mind so you may experience a continual state of gratitude.

The subconscious mind is where all the power of the brain resides. It is the aspect of our brain function that controls roughly 95 percent of the *automated programs* that run our lives, such as walking, driving, breathing, fearing, and loving.

Your conscious mind is your thinking and learning mind, but it has nothing to do with helping you get your daily activities done until your thoughts become ingrained in your biology. The subconscious only "learns" through constant engagement that makes permanent connections between different neurons. To build neural networks that are sufficiently stable and powerful enough to change your subjective view of life, you must practice the same habits and skills day in and day out.

Never doubt for a moment how a small action that is done on a daily basis can give you big results.

The purpose of the FMTG system is to help you establish and sustain new synaptic connections related to the habit of gratitude so that gratitude becomes an empowering new *program* in your subconscious mind. The act of learning this new information and applying it on a daily basis in the ways I am going to be asking you to do—by personalizing it, demonstrating it, and rehearsing it—will help you make the actions of gratitude so familiar to your body and mind that it becomes second nature.

At least, that is the hope I have for you, as it has been the case for many people who have applied it in their lives. I believe FMTG can turn up the dial on your happiness "barometer" and improve your relationships, immunity, and moods.

My system is easy as well as effective because it's geared to complement the busy lives that we all lead. It does not take much effort—in fact, it only requires five minutes of your attention. Of course, if you decide to stay immersed in gratitude longer or to immerse yourself several times a day, you can. Gratitude is perpetually available to everyone because it is part of your human blueprint. Best of all, the power of gratitude is *free*.

Too good to be true? Try it. You have nothing to lose and everything to gain. FMTG could be as life-changing for you as it was for me and the hundreds of Gratituders who have tried it through my program.

Why might FMTG be the single most important thing you can do to change your life for the better? Because spending five minutes each morning in gratitude sets the tone for the rest of the day. It is like a pebble you drop in the water of your soul whose ripple gently touches all areas of your personal and professional life.

I know you are a person who feels grateful—I do not doubt that for a minute. The key to FMTG's impact is that it does more for you than experiencing gratitude once in a while, spontaneously or unexpectedly, when something good happens. It helps you make the attitude of gratitude a permanent part of your personality and the way your brain functions.

The entire purpose of FMTG is to help you remove judgment from any given situation you might be tempted to categorize as being good or bad, fair or unfair, and have you *become* a person who remains in a state of grateful living regardless of your circumstances.

What Is Involved in Practicing the FMTG System?

To maximize your success, I have broken the FMTG system into simple steps. These small daily actions that I prescribe will help you create a powerful new habit. The FMTG practice consists of doing:

- A five-minute routine of focusing on gratitude for a particular topic,

- Once daily—ideally at the same time every day,
- While you are still in bed—either lying down or sitting up—, and
- Making a twenty-eight-day-in-a-row commitment.

Setting Up Your Alarm Helper

In preparation for the morning, please set the alarm to go off five minutes before the time you would normally need to wake up in the morning. Also, program a snooze alert for five minutes after that. The alarm will be your signal to immerse yourself in gratitude. The snooze alert will be your cue that you are done. Waking up a few minutes early means that you don't need to feel pressed for time because you are allocating five extra minutes to your morning routine.

You are not taking any time from your active day. Should you wish to spend longer than five minutes in any of the daily meditations, doing so is entirely up to your time availability.

Make sure to program your alarm to ring at the same time each day of the week since you will be doing this for twenty-eight days straight.

As an example, my day begins at 5:30 AM, so I set my alarm for 5:25 AM and my alert for 5:30. My body is now conditioned to waking at this time that an alarm is no longer necessary, but I still like hearing the alert indicating when to start my practice.

How This Book Is Structured

The FMTG system is structured in weeks—four in total—and includes daily lessons and exercises. Each week is designed in perfect sequence with one lesson building from the previous lessons. As a first-timer, I recommend that you follow the sequence without alteration. The FMTG system is a multiphase healing process designed to uncover the layers of your soul one by one, from the triggers that lay on the surface to the deeper wounds in the recess of your being. Jumping to a random week or day will not work.

- Week One is designed to teach your body to be grateful for having a life and all the blessings it entails.
- Week Two is designed to teach you about the energy and vibration of the emotions, thoughts, and beliefs that led you to attract the life you've had so far and to accept responsibility for what you've created.
- Week Three is designed to bring to the surface all that needs healing in your past and current life so you may free your body of trapped emotions. It is designed to help you peel the layers beyond those you thought were done, allowing you to heal some more.
- Week Four is designed to help you apply all the energy you have freed towards visualizing and creating a new self and the future life of your dreams that you wish to manifest.

Protecting Your Mental Receptivity

It's important that you practice the FMTG routine at the same time and in the same location every day if you can. I recommend first thing in the morning before you leave your bed. If you are traveling, that's OK. Practice FMTG while lying or seated in your hotel bed.

I know insistence on first thing in the morning may sound strange, but science has shown that the subconscious is easiest to access right before and right after sleeping.[2] To maximize your results, it's important to imprint your brain with gratitude before you have the chance to think of anything stressful that could occur during the day ahead.

Please refrain from touching your phone and checking your social media or emails. Yes, your coffee can also wait. *It's just five minutes!*

In order to preserve your mental freshness and receptivity in the morning, I suggest that you read the lesson for what you are supposed to do in the morning the night before. That way, you can concentrate on doing what you need to do one day at a time. There are daily guided meditations that you can when you enroll in an FMTG course, each corresponding to each day of the week to help you through your morning routine if you wish; otherwise, you can do the exercises completely on your own.

If you prefer, you may choose to read the instructions for the entire week at one go. But please refresh your memory of the topic. At the end of the book, I have provided you with a list of all the daily topics, "Twenty-Eight Days of Gratitude at a Glance," to serve as a quick reminder.

The choice is yours.

Visit my website, www.WaleuskaLazo.com/bookgift, to get a free guided audio meditation.

If you are anything like me, understanding the *why* of things makes the *how* seem more possible. For this reason, I advise you to give the FMTG lessons a full reading before you begin so you can understand what the purpose of the methodology for each day.

My favorite protocol is this: Once you have a good grasp of what you will be doing and the sorts of effect you can expect, read the individual day the night before. Keeping the book on your night table where it is handy is also a good idea. I have provided you a "Reflections" space at the end of each day so that you can write about your experience with each area of your FMTG. At the end of the day, before turning out the light and resting your head on the pillow, jot down some notes about the great-fullness you experienced. Writing about your experience and the things you notice throughout the day during the month of FMTG will reinforce your synaptic connections.

FMTG, while it is simple, is also an evolving system. Each consecutive day, the same rules apply. The only thing that changes is the area of your life on which you focus. As the days and weeks go by and the FMTG habit is more firmly established, I will suggest small additional steps that will deepen your practice and will make it even more effective and powerful. Many people go through it more than once and discover new benefits each time they circle back.

One last thing, to enhance your experience, I advise that you join the FMTG Community group on Facebook (see Resources), which is available to everyone who has purchased this book or taken one of the online FMTG Courses. The FMTG online community is a great support system that allows you to interact and pose questions to other people from around the world in a nonjudgmental environment. A lot of the healing you may be seeking can be enhanced by the simple virtue of being in the company of high vibration people (you will learn about vibrations in Week Two) who have come together with one common goal: to exercise gratitude as part of their daily existence.

Two additional advantages of being part of the FMTG Community of Gratituders, which is my name for members of the group, is that you can interact with me there and beta-test new FMTG exercises before they are made available to the general public. Once you become a member of my mailing list and the Gratitude Community, you will be informed of the many webinars I offer all year round to help you during your journey of transformation.

Now that we have the instructions out of the way, *are you ready to transform your life?*

Let's do it!

INVITATION

As a new owner of *The Gratitude Blueprint*, I invite you to take an FMTG program (currently valued at $97USD) for no additional cost as my way of helping you immerse in gratitude and take the work of this book to an even more meaningful level. (Offer for limited time only.)

In the FMTG online course, you will be going through the lessons of this book along with others from around the world at the same time. This will help you keep accountable and ensure completion. Once you purchase your book, go to www.Waleuskalazo.com and visit "FMTG Online Course" so you can check the calendar year for all the possible cohorts you can join, should you wish to do so. The FMTG program runs a few times a year and all you must do is to register for the group you would you like to join.

Once you have joined, you will be put in a cohort with others and you will receive access to twenty-eight guided meditations that go with each day of the lessons in this book. You will have access to me and other mentors of the course who will be happy to help and guide you.

Let me be clear, you do not need to do this. Should you wish to just do the program on your own using the book for guidance, that is perfectly fine. However, I am extending an invitation to you for added value. Many people enjoy the experience of doing the daily lessons and sharing insights and observations with others going through the same process.

Either way, the choice is yours. I look forward to seeing you in one of the FMTG cohorts!

WEEK ONE

*YOU WON'T BECOME HAPPIER BY
HAVING MORE AND NEWER
THINGS. YOU'LL BECOME HAPPIER
BY BEING GRATEFUL FOR THE
THINGS YOU ALREADY HAVE.*

Welcome to the first week of a practice that is the blueprint for a more joyful, peaceful, and happy life.

This week you're going to experience the power of starting every day feeling grateful. Thoughts and emotions create chemical surges in our bodies, so feeding your mind positive thoughts and emotions first thing in the morning will initiate a chemical chain reaction. This practice signals your body to produce more "happy" chemicals. If you do this practice every day, you will undergo a personal transformation. You have the power in your body and the plan in your hands.

The body is stronger than the mind. If your body is imbued with gratitude as the first order of the day on a consistent basis, then your brain receives the message that wonderful things are happening for you. The big secret is that the body cannot distinguish between an event happening in your mind or an event happening in the world outside of the body. Every thought, word, and emotion you perceive is an actual, real-world event in physiological terms no matter how imaginary or fictional it is.

When the first thing you say upon waking is "Thank you for life, thank you for laughter, thank you for my eyesight, my hearing, and my health" you ignite a beneficial force in your brain and body.

If you are an empirical facts kind of person, one who would like to know the exact details of what your body will go through physiologically as you make the shift to grateful living, you will appreciate the following explanation provided by 1998 Nobel Prize-winning biochemist Robert F. Furchgott.

The moment oxytocin is released into the circulatory system, a switch is flipped on our state of being. It shuts off the lights of anger and aggression. It cools the circuits of fear and anxiety. It lowers the volume in our heads of thoughts of pain and suffering. The only emotion we can feel then is a true love for life. In fact, research has shown that when oxytocin levels are elevated even slightly, it's impossible to hold a grudge. When oxytocin is released into the bloodstream, it signals the release of nitric oxide (aka endothelial-derived relaxing factor or EDFR), which causes our arteries to expand. The heart and brain get more energy from the increased blood flow, so we feel whole and blessed.[1]

In other words, by consistently showing and expressing gratitude, you are accustoming your body to welcome the emotions of joy, compassion, appreciation, and love. Over time, your brain becomes conditioned to produce the chemistry of those emotions for you. You will fall more and more in love with life. Who wouldn't want that?

Can you achieve a state of fulfillment and gratitude in only five minutes a day? Yes! —the hundreds of Gratituders in the Gratitude Experiment and I are your living proof. The results I'm describing are not pie-in-the-sky promises. They can be yours. All you need to bring to the table is an open mind and a willing heart.

As you progress through the four weeks of your FMTG practice, you may experience some of the same effects of gratitude that I and the hundreds of others have experienced. I like to refer to these effects as the *lesses and mores*. Among them, you can expect (though they won't be limited to) more calmness, less anxiety, less depression, more overall health and vibrancy, less irritability and reactiveness, less colds and flus, more joy, more attention to details, more appreciation for nature, more acceptance of circumstances and obstacles you are faced with, more curiosity for living, less fear, and more desire to experience adventure. Overall, you'll have more zest for living. As one Gratituder told me, "Since starting FMTG, everything that was wrong is now right in my life. A magical world is opening with a glimpse of what is really out there for me. Once I stopped focusing on the negative—once I am treading water again—I feel new excitement for life."

The Metaphysics of Gratitude

The purpose of your FMTG practice during Week One is to train your body and mind to start the day in a state of gratitude. You will accomplish this over the next seven days by deliberately cultivating gratitude for specific events, things, and people.

A beautiful part of expressing appreciation and love towards others is the secondary effect. Not only do you feel great, but as you do your FMTG practice, your grateful thoughts and feelings emit an energetic signal of love that ripples through the unified field of energy that links all things. In this book, this shall be referred to as *the Field*. Placing your attention on all the people and things you are grateful for will lead energy to flow to the people you think about. In my experience, many will feel your gratitude.

Furthermore, you are not just sending gratitude to a single thing or person, but to the entire Universe—including back to yourself.

Ralph Waldo Emerson once eloquently said, "It is one of the most beautiful compensations of this life that no man can sincerely try to help another without helping himself."[2] I find the same truth applies to gratitude. When we sincerely express gratitude and send love to another person, we are the recipients of love as well.

Every energy we send out comes back to us somehow. This means if you wish peace and joy for another person, you also receive peace and joy. And if you see the good in things and in others, you'll receive goodness. The Universe is like a mirror that reflects the gratitude in your heart back to you.

What does this all mean? It means that when you feel grateful, your heart expands, and you become a magnet for miracles. Some people call this the *law of attraction*. The mere act of saying thanks in advance signals to the Universe that the act of receiving whatever it is you are giving gratitude for or wish to attract has already happened. The Universe, in turn, registers your emotion of gratitude, and like a mirror, she sends more of the same back to you, entering into a state of receivership.

Energy flows where attention goes. If you put your attention on feeling grateful for your life, you are attracting energy to flow to you from which you can do amazing things. In this way, gratitude can bring you a new sense of vitality and empowerment. This can also do wonders for your health! Some people, and I'm one of them, have seen health issues reduced or eliminated while practicing gratitude. How can this happen? I believe that gratitude reduces stress, and it has a vitalizing effect from a positive energy flow.

The magnifying effect of focusing your attention is more than metaphysics. It's also how the brain works with thoughts. Your brain notices what you are focused on and then looks for more of the same things for you out in the world. As an example, suppose you bought a red car. Chances are you see red cars everywhere. Did the red cars magically appear out of nowhere? No. The red cars were always there. The scientific term for this is *reticular activation*. Once your brain is aware of your focus, it no longer filters out red cars. Instead, your brain includes red cars in your field of vision.

Focus on what is good, and you will see more good things. Focus on things for which you feel grateful, and you will see more things that evoke gratefulness in you. Personally, I don't believe that science and metaphysics need to be necessarily exclusive from each other.

Give Your New Routine a Chance

Do not worry if all this seems strange to you at the beginning. Some Gratituders—people who have gone through this system—reported feeling intense resistance and frustration at the beginning. Some Gratituders kept falling asleep. Some could not obtain a connection to gratitude. The minds of others went blank. Those experiences are normal. The important thing is not to get discouraged and give up too soon.

If you feel any resistance, then it means you are doing this correctly. Your subconscious mind may need time to adjust to your new morning routine, but it does adjust. Soon this practice will become a habit, and any initial resistance will be a distant memory. As a course participant reported, "The first week was difficult. But as time passed, something shifted. I've had a much easier time feeling elevated emotions. This program works, but you *must* be persistent and not give up."

The big idea here is to practice giving thanks until it becomes so automatic that you are running around in a constant and effortless state of appreciation for life. Gratitude will be on autopilot for you, just as walking, running, riding a bicycle, or driving a car is for you right now.

Remember, however, that you cannot skip a day. For this habit to become a program in your subconscious mind, you need to exert consistent effort and employ lots of repetition and focus. Daily repetition ensures that neural connections, pathways, and networks form. The time and effort are worth it as the emotional rewards are unbeatable. As one of my Gratituders shares, "I love plugging into feelings of gratitude each morning. It's now become a natural part of me embracing the day."

Ready to create the most powerful habit of your life? Turn the page.

DAY 1

GRATITUDE

PURPOSE: *TO GET COMFORTABLE WITH THE ACT OF GIVING THANKS.*

Today and every day after, start by closing your eyes. It is important to keep them closed for the entire five (or more) minutes that you are practicing FMTG. The reason? Your brain will encounter less sensory information. With less information to filter, your mind can relax and turn inward quicker.

With your eyes closed, think of anything in your life that you can be thankful for. Anything you value. Don't worry about what comes to mind. And don't feel that you must limit yourself to one thing. At first, you are most likely to start with the obvious and broader things, such as your family, your job, your friends, or your health.

That's good. You should be grateful for those types of things. With your eyes closed, say, *"I am thankful for my children (if you have some). I am grateful for my parents, for my lover, for my health. I am grateful for the job that I have and the friends that surround me. I am thankful to have love in my life. I am grateful for the essential necessities that allow me to live comfortably. I am grateful that I have eyes to see the faces of those I love. I am grateful that I can hear and that I can feel the warm embrace of others. I am grateful for touch and that I can kiss the lips of the one who connects my soul."*

This day is meant to be effortless, so just stay in your bed, comfy under your sheets and blankets, and say thanks for anything that happens to pop up. Don't worry at all about what comes out. If it's silly, don't judge it. Just go with it and get used to feeling the sensations of gratitude in your body.

If you have a difficult time concentrating or coming up with enough things to cover in five minutes, don't worry. This is normal.

Relax. It is only your first day. As you practice this routine, it will become easier.

My students report an even split. Some speak of having so many things to express thanks for that five minutes on Day 1 is not enough. Others say that the first five minutes felt eternal, and they could not focus their busy mind. All experiences are part of the process. You are not alone. Relax, and don't force it. You can trust the process.

When you have completed your five minutes, I invite you always to end your FMTG practice by expressing your gratitude with something like, *"I am thankful to the Universe for all my blessings."*

DAY 1 REFLECTIONS

Use this space to write down any thoughts about your experience with gratitude on Day 1. Recording your insights and emotions will imprint gratefulness on your body and mind.

_____

_____

_____

_____

_____

_____

_____

_____

_____

_____

_____

_____

_____

_____

_____

_____

_____

DAY 2

YOUR IMMEDIATE
SURROUNDINGS

PURPOSE: *TO REALIZE JUST HOW MUCH THERE IS TO BE
GRATEFUL FOR IN THE WORLD.*

Yesterday, you experienced what it was like to be thankful. Your focus was broad and general. Today, and on each successive day of the FMTG program, you will practice doing *targeted* or *focused* energy work. In essence, that is what happens when you concentrate your appreciation for someone or something: You direct positive energy to flow where you place your attention.

Today, you will focus on the details of your surroundings. Close your eyes as you focus on your gratefulness for all the things in your space that you like, and as you identify each thing, bring it into your heart. The things you focus on can be your soft mattress, bedding, and pillows, and the shelter of your warm home on a cold winter's day or air conditioning on a sweltering summer morning. Considering how many people are homeless and live on the streets, having a roof over your head is a blessing.

Be grateful for your car, if you have one, which takes you places without having to wait in the cold for a bus to come. I remember growing up in Toronto without a car and freezing outside when I waited for the bus to take me to work or home. The winter months were brutal, and there were days I could not feel my hands and feet regardless of how thick the gloves or the boots I wore were. Now that I have the privilege of driving in a warm car, I am so grateful. When I drive past a bus stop late at night and see people waiting there, I remember the bitter sensation of cold air on my skin.

If you are someone who rides the bus, be grateful that this transportation takes you where you want to go, so you get there safely and do not have to walk from place to place.

How about being grateful for the meals you eat, the warm shower that keeps you clean, or the fact that you have fresh water to drink. Over a billion people on our planet have no clean water to drink, and two and a half billion don't have indoor toilets. Can you see how fortunate you are? Use your FMTG practice today to express gratitude for your plumbing and the municipal water supply.

I was recently in Tulum, Mexico, at a wonderful resort, and I could not flush any toilet paper down the toilet. I also couldn't use their tap water to brush my teeth. This experience made me appreciate what I take for granted at home.

Be thankful for the clothing you wear and the many choices of garment you have. When I first arrived in Canada with my family as refugees from Nicaragua, we had no money and could not afford to buy winter clothing. In preparation for the cold winter, we went to a second-hand store to buy jackets and ice skates for my brothers, who were little boys. When I think back to those days, I remember how even though the things we bought were used, we felt so grateful for our find. My children have experienced none of the hardships I went through as an immigrant, and that is another thing for which I feel extremely grateful. I am grateful that I can give my children the things they need and want.

Focus on all the things that surround you and breathe in gratitude for them. What are the things you never thought about that you take for granted in your home? Do you have electricity? Two billion people in the world have no electricity. Could you be thankful that when you click on a light switch, without giving it any thought or effort, a light comes on as expected? Isn't that something to feel thankful for? Be grateful for the lightbulbs and electricity that enable you to see at night.

I remember the times when my neighborhood lost power from winter storms or power outages. I cannot tell you how crazy I went as I was waiting for the power to return. The one hour spent without power felt like an entire day because I couldn't charge my computer or telephone. Losing power in a storm makes you realize how reliant we have become on the conveniences of our modern era.

After giving thanks for the convenience of her home, a Gratituder reported, "This was a beautiful exercise. I am inclined to take so much for granted. It is beautiful to sit and think about all the blessings that surround me."

The next time you complain about having too much laundry to do, stop, and turn your perspective around. Having laundry means having clothes to wear. I used to complain on Friday nights about the mess in the kitchen after our Shabbat dinners when the dishes were piled high in the sink. Using FMTG, I turned it around: Piles of dishes meant having lots of food to eat. The mess and the noise the kids created made me grateful that my family was having a great time at my home.

Stopping mid-complaint is crucial to peace. As a Gratituder said, "I was getting dressed when I saw my daughter had left a pair of pants on the floor, so I started complaining. Remembering my FMTG, I then said, 'Better to be thankful for having those pants.'"

My point is this: It is too easy for us to go through life not being entirely conscious of our blessings. Change this by becoming aware of how fortunate you truly are in today's FMTG practice. When you have completed this exercise, close your FMTG by expressing your gratitude. You could say something like, "I am thankful to the Universe for surrounding me with all the things that give me abundant comfort. Thank you for I am blessed."

Next time you are having a shitty day, and you feel like nothing is going right for you, it will be that much easier to shift your attention to just how much you actually have in your life that is going right for you. Another student said, "Thank you for opening my eyes to see how fortunate I am. This has shifted my perspective—the little things are not that little and really helps me to feel blessed."

Perspective is a beautiful thing, isn't it?

DAY 2 REFLECTIONS

Use this space to write down any thoughts about your experience with gratitude on Day 2.

_____

_____

_____

_____

_____

_____

_____

_____

_____

_____

_____

_____

_____

_____

DAY 3

NATURE AND OUR PLANET

PURPOSE: *TO REALIZE YOU ARE PART OF SOMETHING MUCH GREATER THAN YOURSELF.*

Welcome to Day 3. Today is the only day we will deviate from the routine this week. Rather than staying in your bed while you do your FMTG practice, I invite you to go outside to your backyard, balcony, front porch, or to sit wherever else you can be in the presence of nature. If you can sit on the grass, even better. If you are unable to go outside, go near a window where you can see the sky. Should none of these recommendations be possible, stay in your bed and envision that you are outdoors connecting with nature.

Today, you will dedicate your FMTG practice to the planet and environment. Aim to be mindful of all the things you miss seeing when you are too busy running against the clock trying to meet the hectic demands of your day.

The purpose of the FMTG practice is to connect to the fact that you are part of something bigger than you. Here the FMTG will help you realize that you are linked to everything in creation. You are one with the Universe. So, close your eyes, start to bring the images of things you are grateful for to your heart, and give thanks for the shining sun that warms your cold mornings. Be grateful for the moon that lights up your night, for the trees that give you shade, and for the chirping birds that announce the dawn. Say, *"I am thankful for all the things nature gives me to thrive and survive."*

Depending on where you are from, you could say:

"I am grateful for the powerful blue ocean and the soothing sounds of its waves."

"I am grateful for the white snow and how beautiful it looks when it has freshly fallen."

"I am grateful for the smell of the earth after it rains."

"I am grateful for the sound of rain when I leave my window open at night."

"I am grateful for the sensation of my bare feet on cool grass on a hot summer day."

"I am grateful to witness a shooting star and make a wish."

"I am grateful for the colors of a butterfly and the beauty of fireflies shimmering in the darkness of night."

"I am grateful for the beautiful moonlight reflected on a lake."

Later, when you go about your day, make a point to walk in nature. Notice the green grass—even stand barefoot on it for a few minutes if you can—and feel grateful for your connection to the earth.

Did you know that a few minutes of grounding like this has healing properties? Touching the soil with your bare feet can boost your energy, reduce inflammation, and strengthen your immune system due to having physical contact with the electrons of the Earth. Isn't that amazing? Say, *"I am grateful for Mother Earth."*

Pick up a dandelion and blow on it and see the magic that it creates. Feel gratitude for the wind on your face and the blue sky above you, and realize that you are part of nature, one with the Earth. Give thanks for the fresh, clean air you are fortunate to enjoy. There is so much to feel grateful for when you pay attention to the beauty and details of the environment around you. If you focus on your gratitude on nature, you will learn to see everything as a miracle.

Mindfulness is an incredible byproduct of the FMTG practice. It is my hope that after expressing gratefulness for our planet, you will begin to stop each night and notice the moon. I hope you will make a point to look at the sun and say thank you the next time you walk down the street. The experience can change your entire outlook on the world and the weather.

A Gratituder sent me a message saying, "I slowly got out of bed this morning and ventured outside. The cold breeze hit my face like a ball to a bat. Instead of complaining about the stinging cold, I embraced the gratitude of being alive and having the opportunity to live another day. I looked out over my deck and watched the deer and birds as I have done before, but today was different. I saw and appreciated them. I thanked Mother Earth for the beautiful snow, the animals, and even that stupid crowing rooster *again*, which has driven me mad other days. I've noticed how this exercise has grounded and humbled me. I have so much to be thankful for."

Through becoming aware that you and your ecosystem are one, you will begin to develop a deep concern and sense of responsibility for the planet. We love and protect that which we feel is ours. So, this is a wonderful opportunity for you to take ownership of our planet because it is yours. Love the earth enough to protect it, if not for yourself, then for those you love and the generations yet to come.

Do you recognize the miraculous qualities of our planet? Think about it for a second. The solar system and galaxy are vast yet so full of moving objects that the chance of something running into our planet is real. There are millions of near-earth objects (NEOs) in outer space that could destroy earth in a blink of an eye, such as asteroids, meteors, and comets, yet don't you find it amazing that somehow our planet manages to dodge them? And here we are, still alive? In fact, small asteroids hit our planet every day. Many more NEOs burn up upon contact with the atmosphere. So, give thanks to Earth's atmosphere for protecting us from a multitude of debris from outer space each day.

According to astronomers, anywhere from 18,000 to 84,000 meteorites bigger than ten grams enter the atmosphere per year.[1] To give you an idea of how small these objects are, consider that a pea weighs .1–.36 grams.

To me, it seems obvious that there is a miracle, a higher power, at work that loves us enough to protect us. That is something we need to be thankful for.

Close your FMTG practice by expressing your appreciation. As an example, you could say, *"I am thankful to the Universe for having me be part of such a miracle."*

DAY 3 REFLECTIONS

Use this space to write down any thoughts about your experience with gratitude on Day 3.

_____

_____

_____

_____

_____

_____

_____

_____

_____

_____

_____

_____

_____

_____

_____

_____

_____

_____

DAY 4

YOUR WORK AND
WORKPLACE

PURPOSE: *TO FIND THE GOOD IN THINGS YOU CANNOT
CHANGE RIGHT AWAY.*

W elcome to Day 4. Starting today, you will incorporate the power of your breath into your FMTG practice. After closing your eyes, as you have been doing for the past three days, you will focus on the sound of your breathing for four breaths before bringing an image to your heart. I'd like you to breathe more slowly and deeply than usual. Inhale slowly, listening, and then exhale slowly. This technique signals to your body that you are safe, and there is no reason to be on high alert. Having received the signal that you are calm, your entire nervous system will relax.

If you find that the breathing makes you sleepy again, that is OK. To avoid falling asleep during your FMTG, try sitting upright on the edge of your bed.

Today, you will focus your FMTG on your job and workplace. I know this topic can be sensitive for some people since I hear feedback about it all the time. Some say, "Well, I don't really love my job" or "I am unemployed (or retired)." No matter what your professional circumstances at present may be, if you dig, there is always something to be grateful for. The coronavirus pandemic caused many people to lose their jobs in 2020. In Canada, according to a labor force survey and reported by CBC news, in a matter of one month, two million jobs were lost. In the United States, 20.6 million jobs were lost in one year due to COVID-19. This puts things in perspective! The mere fact of holding a job and having an income to count on is a blessing. Perhaps it's the nice coworkers you have or the people you may talk to on the phone while at work. Whatever it is, there is something that can make you feel thankful. If you are retired or unemployed, focus on your past jobs and what you were grateful for.

The purpose of the FMTG practice is to help you focus on the good and not on what you feel does not work for you. The entire premise of practicing gratefulness is to learn to shift your mindset. Once you see all the things that you could be thankful for, your attitude towards your workplace, colleagues, customers, clients, and job will change. Surprisingly, you may even start to enjoy things about your job that you never did before. As the late Wayne Dyer always used to say, "If you change the way you look at things, the things you look at change."[1]

Your workplace is the place where most adults spend their waking hours. In essence, your work is your home away from home (unless you have a home office). Having negative feelings about your job will only make you discontented and stressed, which, in turn, will reduce the quality of your life.

Use today's FMTG session to shift how you think and feel about the work you do. If you can't change your job, learn to find things in it that you appreciate. You do not have to like every aspect of working, so do your best to find things to be thankful for. Even appreciating small details will help you feel more at peace and joyful.

When you are ready, close your eyes and become aware, for a few seconds, of the sound of your breath as you slowly inhale deeply and exhale. Pay attention to the sensations you feel as air moves in and out of your body. After a few rounds of breathing, begin bringing images of your workplace to your heart.

Even if work is difficult right now, feel gratitude for some aspect of your work while you continue breathing deeply and expressing appreciation in your mind for the work you have.

As an example, you might say, *"I am grateful for holding a job when there are so many people employed. I am grateful for the purpose this work brings to my life. I'm thankful for the friends I've made at work, for the people I meet, for those I can help."* Whatever is true for you, give thanks for it.

If you are not currently working or you are working from home, find things about it that you can be grateful for. Perhaps you are self-employed, and this allows you to spend time at home attending to your children—be grateful for that. Perhaps you are grateful that you can make your own schedule, which gives you greater flexibility to do other things also. If your work has you travel, be grateful for the places you visit. Whatever is true for you, give thanks for it.

After doing this exercise, one of my Gratituders noted, "Giving gratitude this morning for my work environment was timely given that I have been more negative lately for a variety of reasons. My workload has been dragging me down and making me feel drained. I needed to remind myself of all the reasons I have chosen to work where I do, including how working there allows me the flexibility to be a more present mother and wife, which are the most important things to me at this stage of my life. I was happier today at work than I have been in a while."

When you complete your five (or more) minutes of immersion in gratitude, end by expressing gratitude, you could say something like *"I am thankful to the Universe for blessing me with a job and for showing me that even when things aren't as I wish, there still much I am grateful for."*

Whether or not you are the boss in your business, as you go about your day today, focus on things that people do right. Next time you see them, you might mention these things to them. Acknowledge their efforts. Look for the good in everything, and you will find it.

DAY 4 REFLECTIONS

Use this space to write down any thoughts about your
experience with gratitude on Day 4.

_____

_____

_____

_____

_____

_____

_____

_____

_____

_____

_____

_____

_____

_____

_____

_____

_____

_____

_____

_____

_____

_____

DAY 5

YOUR CHILDREN AND OTHER TENDER BEINGS

PURPOSE: *TO PRACTICE SENDING FOCUSED POSITIVE ENERGY TO OTHERS.*

Welcome to Day 5. Today you will dedicate your FMTG to your child or children or grandchildren. If you are not a parent, focus on a niece or nephew, or another child you know and care about. Some people who work professionally with children, such as teachers and sports coaches, use their pupils.

This exercise can be triggering for people who do not have children for a variety of reasons. If this exercise triggers you, embrace it as an opportunity to put your discomfort to rest.

Here are some other ways you might include yourself in today's activity.

- Try acknowledging your inner child or some of the qualities and attributes you liked about yourself when you were a child.
- Alternatively, focus on a pet or a plant that is under your care.
- Or make a list in your mind of all the things you would be grateful for if you had children.

Are you ready for Day 5?

Great!

Focus on the qualities you are thankful for in the child. Maybe the child is kind, creative, resourceful, funny, and determined. For example, I am grateful that my daughters have enormous emotional intelligence. One of them is sensitive to the feelings of the people around her and expresses tremendous empathy. I give gratitude for my child's empathy and for the fact that this quality will serve her well throughout her life. My other daughter has different strengths. She has strong organizational and preparedness skills. She excels academically, for which I am also grateful.

Picture a physical attribute of the child you love and focus on your gratitude for that attribute. I love that my daughter has long, strong legs that are beautiful and muscular, like the legs of a stallion. The strength in these legs makes her a great sprinter and jumper for her school's track and field team. I also love my daughter's hair, which is thick and long, and I admire how beautiful it looks when the wind blows through it. As I am feeling gratitude for her, I picture her cheeks, which are always rosy no matter what she is doing, and I feel such love for each of her physical attributes.

Perhaps your children are agile, fast, and flexible. Imagine how those attributes aid and enhance their lives and experiences. Because it is possible that you have never thought of these things before, the purpose today is to give you a deeper perspective on the gifts and blessings you receive through your children. If your children play a sport, what physical attributes can you link to their successes?

For example, close your eyes and breathe slowly in and out. Think of the way your child is built, and, in your mind, you could say, *"I am grateful that my child has long legs that give the advantage of speed. I am grateful that my child is tall and can jump, which is an advantage in basketball. I am grateful that my child has hand-eye coordination, which serves to excel in tennis,"* or *"I am grateful that my child is strong and built to withstand the tackles in football."*

Whatever you are grateful for, begin to feel grateful for every connection. These are just ideas I am giving you. Don't feel you are limited to expressing thankfulness for the traits and people I am pointing out. Make the practice your own by expressing gratitude for the things that are true and that you admire, such as intelligence, empathy, compassion, altruism, honesty, and respect.

We all have attributes that give us advantages—these are different for each of us—express your gratitude for some of those things. The purpose of today's FMTG is to make you aware of all the blessings you receive through children and their qualities.

One Gratituder, who is a mother, told me, "Until this morning's FMTG, I never realized how critical my mind is programmed to be. Although I love the two beautiful souls I am raising, my focus has consistently been on attributes that need improvement instead of taking notice of the amazing qualities they have that make them unique. I had a breakthrough today that completely altered my frame of mind. Words cannot express the gratitude I feel for this epiphany. Happy tears are flowing this morning."

When you feel you have completed the exercise, proceed to close your FMTG practice by expressing your gratitude. Say something like *"I'm thankful to the Universe for the blessings I receive through my children."*

DAY 5 REFLECTIONS

Use this space to write down any thoughts about your experience with gratitude on Day 5.

_____

_____

_____

_____

_____

_____

_____

_____

_____

_____

_____

_____

_____

_____

_____

_____

_____

_____

_____

_____

_____

_____

_____

_____

_____

DAY 6

YOUR SIGNIFICANT OTHER
(PRESENT OR PAST)

PURPOSE: *TO RECONNECT TO THE FEELINGS AND REASONS THAT FIRST BROUGHT YOU AND A SIGNIFICANT OTHER TOGETHER.*

Today and every day from now on, bring the images of the things and people to whom you are dedicating your FMTG practice to your heart rather than to your mind. This will help you reach a deeper and faster connection with the people in your life.

Ready?

With your eyes closed, begin to breathe slowly in and out. Focus on the sound of every breath for a few counts, and when you're ready, bring the image of your current partner or lover to your heart. If you are not in a relationship, think of any significant other from your past. Or imagine your ideal partner.

Notice that I said to bring the image of your significant other *to your heart* and not your mind. Feel and see it.

Once you have connected to the image of a certain individual, think of the things you are thankful for in this person. A suggestion is to take yourself back to the moment when you first fell in love.

See a clear picture of that moment and bring it to your heart as you run through the emotions you felt when you realized that this person was someone with whom you wanted to spend time.

Do you have that image in your heart? Good.

Now, let your heart feel the admiration you have for the beloved and breathe deeply into that emotion. In your mind, express whatever you wish to this person. For example, you could say, *"Thank you for always being there to support me. Thank you for being my friend and companion."*

Now, think of the qualities you appreciate in your partner. Perhaps your partner has a way of making you feel safe, cared for, significant, or maybe it's the way they kiss you or look at you that you appreciate the most. Whatever it is that comes to mind, say (as an example), *"I am grateful that you are in my life. I am grateful that you choose me each day. I am grateful that there is no one else I would rather be with than you. I am grateful that after a day's work, I come home to you. I am grateful to share my bed with you."*

My phrases are not meant for you to recite unless they resonate with what you feel. The phrases are simply prompts intended to trigger your creativity. Say whatever is true for you.

It is my hope that this exercise will reconnect you to your loved one so that you can appreciate what he or she means to you. After doing this exercise, one of my Gratituders said, "I've been married twenty-five years, nearly half my life. Yes, there are times when things are mundane, and I take him for granted. Yes, there are times when he gets on my nerves. Yes, there are times when I fleetingly wonder if my life would be better without him or if I had never met him. This morning I found it therapeutic to pare the years and remember why I married him. A combination of serendipity and synchronicity brought us together—a blind date from a lonely heart column. Giving concentrated gratitude to him for those moments, I realize that a combination of love and respect has kept us together. I am grateful to the Universe."

Something beautiful occurs when we go inward to express our gratitude for those closest to us. Whatever anger you may be feeling or felt in the past for your partner, no matter if you are feeling disconnected, I guarantee that it will dissipate as you reflect on qualities in them that you appreciate. Only one emotion can prevail at any given moment, so, no matter what you have been feeling, it will now be replaced with appreciation as you do today's FMTG.

Whatever hardships you may be facing at the moment, let them go. For five minutes, focus solely on the great moments you have had that made you smile. As one of my students said, "Doing this wonderful exercise brought a sense of absolute love over me and feelings of unity that I knew we have but which I had not felt for him in a while."

Where did you go on your first date? What songs did you dance to? How did you make each other laugh? Remember your first kiss or the first time you made love and breathe gratitude into that moment. You can feel that same emotion today. All you need to do is focus on gratitude for each day you have together. If you do that, you will realize how much precious time has been wasted being upset about things that, in the grand scheme of life, don't even matter. What matters is the privilege to have someone you love to wake up to each morning.

Another Gratituder told me, "This morning's gratitude practice has been absolutely mind-blowing for me. It has completely cleared out any petty resentments and doubts that I have had around my marriage. Focusing on the beginning of the relationship and all the amazing qualities that my husband has is making me feel so very much in love with him again. I can't state enough how grateful I am for this FMTG. It's hard to comprehend how spending five minutes being grateful is having such a life-changing effect on me. I'm grateful."

Once you complete your FMTG, close your practice by expressing your gratitude for your blessings. You could say something like *"I am thankful to the Universe for all the love, adventures, and memories I've been blessed to experience with my partner."*

I often hear couples say, "Marriage is difficult." Having learned what I did from my own marriage, my response is,

"Yes, marriage can be difficult, but it can also hold blessings. It all depends on what you choose to focus on."

DAY 6 REFLECTIONS

Use this space to write down any thoughts about your experience with gratitude on Day 6.

_____

_____

_____

_____

_____

_____

_____

_____

_____

_____

_____

_____

_____

_____

_____

_____

_____

_____

_____

_____

DAY 7

YOUR PARENTS

PURPOSE: *TO REALIZE THAT PARENTS DO WHAT THEY CAN WITH WHAT THEY KNOW.*

Welcome to Day 7. Today marks the conclusion of the first week of your FMTG practice. I hope you have begun to feel and notice the benefits. Today, you will focus on what, for many, has proven a difficult subject: your relationship with your parents.

During the Gratitude Experiment course, some people report that this exercise is a source of appreciation. For many Gratituders, their parents are their champions and nurturers. Others, such as those who have lost their parents, find that this exercise evokes feelings of sadness and loss. Some Gratituders who historically had challenging relationships with their parents say that the exercise has brought up feelings of disappointment. If thinking about your parents is uncomfortable, it is my hope that doing this exercise brings to the surface all the things you need to heal and things you may have forgotten that you can be appreciative for.

One more thing. Repeating this particular exercise is one that has benefited many, helping them heal wounds that were stored deep in their subconscious minds. Five minutes, while useful to get connected to deep-rooted emotions and memories, may not be enough time to heal what needs to be fully healed. So, spend as long as you need to on this exercise.

Alternatively, depending on your circumstances with your parents, you could spend a few days repeating this exercise and healing all the events of your past and childhood with your parents. Once you have healed what needs to be healed, you'll be able to think of your parents and give gratitude without feeling triggered. After that, you may proceed with Week Two.

Are you ready to dedicate this FMTG to your parents?

Great!

By now, you know the drill. Close your eyes and focus on your breath going in and out slowly, while also bringing the image of your parents or a caregiver you had in childhood into your heart. Think of all the reasons, big or small, on why you feel grateful for them.

As you focus on the things they have done for and with you over the years, you could say, *"I am grateful for your restless protection, for your infinite love, for your unconditional support. Thank you for always putting my needs in front of your own. Thank you for knowing what I need even before I do."*

Say what it feels true for you, of course. But if you need a little help to trigger your thoughts, here are some more examples. You could say:

"Thank you for your sacrifice to make sure I wanted for nothing."

"Thank you for worrying about me."

"Thank you for making me feel special and for encouraging me to follow my dreams."

"Thank you for giving me your undivided attention and letting me have that last piece of pie while pretending you did not want it."

"Thank you for your advice and wisdom even in the moments when I did not ask for it and thought I didn't need it."

"Thank you for building my confidence."

"Thank you for celebrating my every accomplishment and for cheering me on at every stage."

If your circumstances were different, you could say, *"Thank you for providing me an education, a home, and a meal for me. I am thankful that although you were not always there for me, this forced me to become self-sufficient, independent, and courageous. Thank you because your neglect made me a stronger and more resourceful person."*

Never feel compelled to use the same phrases I am using. I am simply providing you options.

If my suggestion resonates with you about your relationship with your parents in your younger years, you could say, *"Thank you for tucking me in at night, thank you for every dropoff, for being my driver, doctor, teacher, and coach. Thank you for raising me to be all I could be. Thank you for believing in me even in the moments when I doubted myself. Thank you for being my pillar, my moral compass, and the foundation I used to build who I am."*

If you feel the parenting you received was neglectful or abusive or you were orphaned or raised in foster care, do your best to find something to appreciate. Remember that you don't have to like everything you experienced, but your job for the next five minutes is to put aside those things and focus solely on something you can appreciate. Express gratefulness in words and with images that are true for you. Maybe you could be grateful for your parents or caregiver putting a roof over your head and food on the table.

Maybe your parents are no longer alive. Still, you can give thanks to them for their legacy and love. Be grateful for being given your life. Be grateful that you were made from an act of love. If your parents adopted you, be grateful that they chose to welcome you into their family.

Also, I invite you to consider that your parents were victims of their own upbringings and often did things because that was the only way they knew how to do them. We may not see eye to eye with those who raised us, but we can find the gratitude we are seeking in knowing that no matter how they acted when we were little, they were perhaps acting out of fear that something bad might happen to you. Have compassion. We often judge our caregivers harshly until we become parents ourselves. Babies don't come with manuals on how to parent them. That is something parents learn mostly by trial and error. Giving slack to your parents when they don't do things quite the way you would like might ease tension in your relationship.

It is not always easy to appreciate or even notice what our parents do or did for us. Sometimes we take parents for granted because they have always been there, and unconsciously we believe they will continue to be there for us no matter what. Today, I also encourage you to think about your expectations of them. Hopefully, the next time you're with your parents, you will be able to express your gratitude in person as you are doing now through this exercise.

I did not have a close relationship with my mother as a child. In fact, for many years I believed that my mother didn't love me, or at least not as much as my brothers. Unfortunately, our personalities clashed, so we could never seem to find common ground. I suffered pain because of this. I built a wall around me and carried a burden for over forty years, feeling the absence of the most important bond a child can have with the person who was supposed to be the closest to her. It was not until I started to practice FMTG that my relationship with my mother changed. That was when, instead of remembering all the arguments and differences between us when I thought of my mother, I shifted my focus to her positive attributes. Because I was no longer thinking about what I missed from her, I was able to find the gifts in our relationship. I found compassion, understanding, and forgiveness.

This is not to excuse what some parents do to their children—of course not. However, it can be more resourceful for us to recognize that the harmful ways our parents may have acted towards us are the only ways they knew how to act. As one of my Gratituders said, "This FMTG exercise made me realized that the kind of relationship I wish I could have had with my parents, I will never get because they cannot give what they don't know how to give. However, in looking for gratitude and purpose, I see now that this experience is what made me decide that I would do better and have a better relationship with my children. I will not let them suffer or hurt the way I had. Thank you for the wisdom. Today I have cried, and I even felt love for my parents."

We all have traumas we are dealing with, and our parents were/are no different. While I cannot even begin to understand the pain someone who has been molested or physically hit by a parent has felt, the gratitude can be found in your own realization that the action taken could not have come from a healthy, conscious person. The FMTG is looking for gratitude—and perhaps for being able to forgive and to understand just how wounded that person was. FMTG can also help you put into perspective that perhaps, culturally, some parents think that hitting their children is a right they have. You can be grateful that, in spite of the pain, you made it through, and you are strong enough to forgive so you are not enslaved to your past trauma.

One Gratituder who posted her reflections in the FMTG community wrote, "This morning's FMTG was a tough one as it brought back trauma from earliest memory's inflicted by my own parents. I forgive them for not having a better understanding of the damage they were causing. I forgive them for being weak in times of anger and frustration. I am grateful for them giving me life. I am grateful that my past taught me how to be a strong, resilient person. My traumas in my childhood allowed me to give everything of myself as a parent to my children. Writing this was not easy. I cannot stop the tears from flowing. I am grateful for my big, open heart, which enables me to see the purpose and to forgive."

For me, it was the realization that my mother behaved in the only manner she knew how that helped me to find the compassion and forgiveness necessary to amend our bruised and damaged relationship. Through immersing myself in gratitude for my mother, I was able to connect with some memories I had suppressed.

Today I feel thankful to have been raised by a woman who worked tirelessly for her children. My mother is a woman who sacrificed her happiness to stay in a marriage that was no longer serving her. She did this because, for her, it was important that her children had a complete family. Today I am grateful for the commitment, dedication, and love my mother shows for my children. My children have the best grandma in the world, and they are as crazy about her as she is about them.

Another blessing of the Day 7 FMTG practice is that it allowed me to learn what not to do with my children. I learned to love each of my girls not in the way I thought they ought to be loved, but in the manner in which each of my daughters needs to be loved. I may not be a "perfect" parent, because I make mistakes, but I do know to ask myself one important question: *"Am I the kind of mom I would have liked to have had?"*

If the answer is yes, then that is good enough for me.

Something positive can be derived from any relationship, and I hope you are able to find it through this exercise. Once you have completed your FMTG, don't forget to close your practice by expressing your gratitude. You could end by saying something like this: *"I am thankful to the Universe for the parents I was given. I am accepting of the love, the lessons, and the understating of the circumstances. Thank you for the perspective."*

DAY 7 REFLECTIONS

Use this space to write down any thoughts about your experience with gratitude on Day 7.

_____

_____

_____

_____

_____

_____

_____

_____

_____

_____

_____

WEEK TWO

ENJOY EACH MOMENT AS THE MIRACLE IT IS.

Congratulations on completing FMTG Week One. Many of the Gratituders reported feeling calmer at this point. Like them, during the first few days, you may have experienced that five minutes felt like an eternity, and you could not concentrate on giving thanks. But then, towards the end of the week, they felt that five minutes just wasn't enough time for them to express all their gratefulness. I loved hearing that.

Anytime you learn something new, it's normal to feel that time stretches if some resistance appears. In the contemporary world, we are also not accustomed to silence. We often grab our smartphones to start texting or responding to overnight emails practically the moment we wake. So, if you are experiencing resistance to spending five minutes immersing yourself silently in gratitude, don't stress about it. It's completely predictable. In fact, if you didn't encounter some resistance, I would say you weren't doing your FMTG correctly.

It is not unusual to find it mentally or emotionally challenging to get into the right frame of mind. But I assure you, a new state of mind will come with practice.

It is also not unusual, even common, to experience some regret as you practice expressing gratitude for different days' topics. Be kind to yourself as any sadness, anger, guilt, or shame arises. Let the feelings pass through your emotional system unimpeded. In order to heal, you must allow yourself to feel your emotions, as bypassing them can only lead to deeper turmoil.

Many of my Gratituders report that starting the day in gratitude allows them to progress through their activities with more ease, calmness, and lightness. But sometimes, people feel a little worse before they feel better. As one Gratituder said, "The second week hit me hard. It was an emotional detox, but I am so glad I pushed through it. It has made me aware of things people tend to hide away in ourselves, whether it's because the trauma is so bad and debilitating that we think it's best to stow it away in the back of our minds or because of our own egos, which don't want us to know anything different. The hidden stuff creates a terrible imbalance. Having this chance to work through my backlogged emotions was immeasurably valuable."

Another Gratituder said, "I find the five minutes of thought, reflection, or just being still, subtly powerful, and it impacts my mindset for the day. I am now so aware of how much I had not been grateful for that I noticed the other day that I have been going to bed earlier because I look forward to waking up to do my FMTG. It is a beautiful, energizing experience."

I love hearing how people's lives are being transformed by them, rewiring their brains for perpetual gratefulness with FMTG. Another student wrote me, saying, "I'm so pleased with this system, and I love its structure, from looking from within towards important matters inside us to looking outward towards children, spouse, work, surroundings, nature, and parents. I'm enjoying the five minutes of meditation in the morning; however, I'm noticing that similar five-minute opportunities also pop up spontaneously throughout the day when I'm doing chores, working, or driving."

Now, I am excited to introduce you to the deeper practice for Week Two. Over the next seven days, you will learn about the power of energy and how it relates to you and your life.

Energy Frequencies

Everything in the Universe—every living thing, sound, emotion, and thought—is made of energy that moves in waves. Each wave has a specific frequency. This means that *you* are like a mini smartphone or radio tower emitting waves of energy that are sent into the atmosphere, and at the same time, you are exposed to waves of energy produced by everything in the world around you.

In 1951, German scientist Winfried Schumann was able to measure the electromagnetic frequency of the Earth, which is in constant communication with us. The Earth's frequency, 7.83 Hertz (Hz.), came to be known as the Schumann resonance.[1] What most fascinates me is that thirty years later, the inventor of the electroencephalogram (EEG) device measured the alpha waves produced in the human brain (alpha waves are associated with a relaxed, awake state) and discovered that they are almost the same, ranging from 8–12 Hz.[2] I was stunned when I learned this, and happy, because it confirms what spiritual teachers and indigenous peoples have been saying for thousands of years: We are one with the Earth. Understanding that the frequency of our thoughts overlaps with the frequency of our planet makes me feel grateful, special, and connected.

Every organ and cell in our bodies has a *voltage* like a tiny battery. According to cell biologist and epigeneticist Bruce Lipton, Ph.D., every live cell in our bodies has 1.4 volts, which may not seem like enough to make a difference. But when you multiple 1.4 volts by 50 trillion, which is the number of cells in the human body, it's clear there are 70 trillion volts of electricity circulating through our bodies constantly, which makes us incredibly powerful generators of electromagnetic energy.[3] Each of us is so powerful, in fact, that we could light up a small village.

Amazing, right?!

It is up to you to choose how to use your energy in your life. As you are learning, states of gratitude and love make it possible for you to direct your electromagnetic force anywhere you want. The purpose of our FMTG practice is to apply that energy to healing our lives.

Dr. Lipton also claims—and this resonates with me—that different frequencies are produced by different states of being, and that the main generators of our frequency at any given moment are our emotions and thoughts.[4] The frequency of each human emotion has been measured, and scientists found they cover a range from as low as 20 Hz. for emotions such as shame, anger, and guilt, to as high as 700 Hz. for gratitude. The frequency of emotions such as love, joy, acceptance, peace, and compassion ranges from 350–550 Hz.[5]

I am not a scientist, so I cannot give you an accurate explanation for how the human mind and body function as they do—and I'm not sure neurologists and biologists even have complete answers yet. What is important to understand in terms of our gratitude practice is that everything that we are made of, from our cells and organs to our emotions and thoughts, produces an electromagnetic field that can be strengthened by positive emotions.

Here's what you need to know. Your emotions can take the energy fields around you and transform these energy fields to vibrate at the same frequency. This is the phenomenon known as *entrainment*.

Your energy field can extend anywhere from ten to fifteen feet from your body, perhaps even farther. To date, however, it is the limitations of our technology that only allow us to measure up to that distance. There are many subtle vibrations that the human senses cannot perceive that affect us.

What does this mean for us in our daily lives? It means that we resonate with anything that is vibrating at the same frequency as us. If we are angry, we will be more attuned to conflict and problems—and other angry people will be attracted to us.

If you are living life controlled by stress, guilt, and operating in survival mode, then it is much harder to attract anything great that you wish to create or attract into your life. If you really want to change your life for the better, you must work on first changing your mental and emotional vibration. Think of your body as both a transmitter and a magnet. You transmit your emotions to the Universe, which in turn, attracts to you people, circumstances, and events that match your frequency.

Trust me! I attracted bad things into my life because, unfortunately, I was living my life at an unhealthy frequency for an extended period of time. I resonated with toxic people, hurtful experiences, and poor health. As a result, I attracted an illness into my life that no doctor or conventional medicine was able to cure. It was not until I learned to change the frequency of my body and my subconscious thoughts using gratefulness that I miraculously began to heal.

Do you see how important it is to practice living in a state of gratitude? If you want to attract great things for your life, learn to stay joyful, peaceful, accepting, loving, forgiving, and grateful. As the Indian mystic Sri Ramakrishna once said, "The winds of God's grace are always blowing; it is for us to raise our sails."[6] I could not agree more with this statement. We don't get lucky by chance but by actively changing the resonance of our emotions.

Do you want to live a more blissful life? Then you must learn to rise above the noise, the confusion, and the illusions in your daily life so you can resonate with the grace of the Universe, which is always available and abundant. When you elevate your frequency, you are drawn closer to the source of miracles.

What is the best way for you to quickly achieve a state of elevated frequency?

Ready for great news? You have been doing it already for a week by establishing the habit of grateful living with your morning FMTG routine. One of the amazing benefits of the practice is that although it only takes five minutes, you will be vibrating at a healthy frequency long after you have done your morning ritual. Without exception, my Gratituders reported feeling more calm, peaceful, and tolerant, and even having better sleep cycles after doing this simple practice for one week.

One Gratituder reported, "I feel really blessed to have been included in this amazing journey called FMTG. It has brought me an awareness of the way to live life. I believe that we are reactive beings living our lives driven by the external stimulus that our senses receive. Now I have become aware of what it feels like to become conscious throughout the day. I feel a different kind of calm and peace that has engulfed my being. I am so much comfortable with everything around me, which would have been a sense of discomfort before I embarked on this wonderful journey. The chatter in my mind has eased. I feel people more. I am more vocal about how happy people make me, and about my love for them. I have found myself saying thank you a lot more, and I speak more lovingly and patiently. Interestingly, a few people have already commented that they can see a change in me."

Each time you feel emotions associated with gratitude and give thanks for things in your life, the frequency of your subtle energy elevates. To increase your chances of tapping into the divine essence of the Universe, you will learn to engage your heart over the next seven days. FMTG works wonders because the heart is the strongest, most powerful generator of electromagnetic waves of any organ in the body.[7]

When you feel your emotions in your heart, and you allow your heart to guide you, you emit powerful waves that are similar to the ones that a person deep in meditation emits. The quickest way I know to achieve this is by placing your hand over your heart and focusing your attention inward to that beautiful organ that beats life into you while engaging in concentrated gratitude for all you have with all your senses.

When we focus on love, compassion, and gratitude in the way the FMTG practice is teaching us to do, a coherent electrical signal of communication between the heart and the brain is established. Scientists have measured this frequency at 0.1 Hz. Gregg Braden, who has written extensively on the science of human potential, reports, "It is so low that it's nearly impossible to hear with our naked ears. This practically imperceptibly frequency is right on the threshold of feeling and hearing. It is also the same frequency whales use to communicate under the ocean."[8]

The moment you start to feel the emotion of gratitude in your body, your mind starts to believe that you are living and experiencing whatever you are thinking about for real in that present moment. I love what Braden advises: "What we choose to experience in our lives, we must first feel in our hearts."[9]

This is precisely what I will guide you through each morning during the coming week. You will wake up putting your focus on your heart, expressing deep appreciation for all you have in your life in a precise sequence that synchronizes your heart and brain to create powerful energy: the signature of love. As you enter a loving state of being, you resonate with loving, positive-minded people and attract harmonious experiences of joy.

A Gratituder describes how shifting his thoughts shifted his life experiences. "My behavior has changed because of my thoughts and how I choose to see things have changed. I choose to see things better now, and the value and meaning I give to things and situations have also changed. I am lighter, softer. Before, I was more rigid and heavy in my thinking. Since I changed, the situations, persons, and relationships in my life also seemed to change for the better."

Second Week Addition to Your FMTG Practice: Incorporating the Energy of Your Heart

Now that you are confident in your practice of the basic FMTG technique, we're going to add another element to the practice: a step of preparation. From now on, I would like you to take a moment at the beginning of your morning ritual to link your heart and brain to create a powerful harmony in your energy field.

Here is what you will need to do.

1. As in Week One, remain lying in your bed after waking with your eyes closed. If you found that you were falling back asleep last week, try sitting up in your bed with your eyes closed.

2. Place your left hand over your heart (or both hands if that works better for you) to drive your energy to it. Through your hand, feel your heart's every beat.

When you connect like this to your heart, it triggers the flow of oxytocin, one of the neurochemicals that make people fall in love. It regulates bonding. Now you are becoming consciously connected to your heart, the organ that beats life into you. If that's not a reason to fall in love with it, I don't know what would be!

3. Begin to breathe slowly and deeply while picturing your heart. Visualize your heart expanding and contracting with every breath you take. Breathe gratitude into it. Do this for at least forty seconds before you get into your practice with the day's topic.

4. With each day of FMTG, focus on the feelings of appreciation, acceptance, gratitude, and love for people and things in your life. Really connect to the source of life as you bring the images of those you are grateful for into your heart.

Remember, you are broadcasting an electromagnetic signature into the Universe with every thought you think that influences every aspect of your life and affects those around you.

Underlying material reality is a field of quantum energy. This field is alive and pulsating and in constant communication with you. It is the same field that is a container wherein all possibilities reside in an infinite number of outcomes. The Field acts as a mirror that reflects back to you the things you subconsciously believe you deserve. So, when you spend time concentrating on gratitude, you are declaring out loud to the Universe that you are thankful, appreciative, and complete. The Field mirrors back to you more of the very life you are giving gratitude for. In simple terms, you become the creator of and magnet for miracles.

Are you ready to elevate your life? Then read on and let's start Week Two.

DAY 1

YOUR CHARACTER-
DEFINING MOMENTS

PURPOSE: *TO REFLECT ON ACTIONS AND DECISIONS THAT
MAKE YOU PROUD TO BE THE PERSON YOU ARE.*

A character-defining moment is any moment when you made a decision between doing right or wrong, or between doing what was easy or hard. Was there ever a time when you did the right thing even if you knew it would prove difficult?

We all have those defining moments; do we not? Some such moments in my life that have been sources of great pride for me, also have been some of the most difficult. One of those moments was the moment I told my former husband after twenty-three years together that I wanted to end our marriage. Although this may sound crazy to you, I walked away out of love for him. It would have been easy for me to stay—after all, the man is one in a billion. I knew I would have a next-to-impossible time finding another man with as much integrity and loyalty. But I'd reached a fork in my road. Out of love for him and myself, I walked away so my husband could find the love he deserved that I, for whatever reason, was unable to provide. That is a moment whose consequences I live with each day. Instead of lamenting on what was lost, I let myself feel pride and love for making this brave decision.

That moment defined my character. I could have stayed in a marriage that made us both unhappy—worse, we might have hurt each other in irreparable ways. But I chose the road less traveled and ended that phase of our relationship with dignity and love. I decided that I wanted to be a woman I could feel proud of when I looked in the mirror. I wanted to be a good example for my daughters. And more than anything, I wanted my ex-husband to remember me as a woman who loved him enough to set him free.

Now that I have given you an example of one of my character-defining moments, I invite you to close your eyes, place your hand over your heart and begin breathing slowly and deeply. Become conscious of your breath while you imagine your beautiful heart expanding and contracting and pumping life-giving blood and energy throughout your body.

One of the beautiful things that will occur as soon as you place your hand on your heart is that you will signal your heart that a shift of your inner state has taken place.

With this one small gesture, you are no longer engaged in the world around you, but you become aware of the world within.

Today, while holding your beautiful heart, the place of your connection with your soul, I invite you to think of a specific event or moment when you took a course of action that caused you to feel proud of yourself. Bring an image of that moment to your heart.

As an example, when I did FMTG for the defining moment I just shared with you, I said, *"Thank you for giving me the courage to live my life from a place of integrity and truth. I am grateful that although we are not together as husband and wife, we still share an unbreakable bond as parents to our children and can express deep caring and compassion for each other."*

As you do your FMTG, say whatever feels good about *your* moment. Perhaps you are finding yourself at a crossroads in a relationship like I was, and it is difficult for you to decide which direction to go. I am a strong believer that true love never ends; it simply transforms. Rather than focusing on what you are losing, try expressing gratitude for the gift of the time you had together—for the lessons, the memories, and the love you shared. If that is the case, you could say, *"I am grateful that I had the courage to walk away from a situation that was unhealthy for me. I am grateful that I loved myself enough to know I deserve more."*

You could choose to think of a moment that defined your character and express your gratitude for it. As an example, you could say, *"I am grateful that instead of overreacting and saying things that I could hurt and later regret, I chose instead to show compassion and peaceful resolution."*

Maybe your defining moment was not letting peer pressure guide you. You could say, *"I am grateful that I stood up for what I believe. I am grateful that I chose to take the road less traveled."*

What was your character-defining moment? When you recall it, breathe through the emotions and send yourself love and compassion for taking your action or making your decision.

If you can't think of a defining moment, but you do remember a moment in which you could have taken a better action and didn't, bring the memory of that to your heart. Give yourself permission to forgive yourself for the decision you made.

In order to move on to better emotions, it is vital that you learn to forgive yourself for outcomes you can no longer change. As a Gratituder said after the Week 2 Day 1 lesson, "I really loved this exercise as I was grateful to be able to forgive myself for moments that defined me that I thought I could have done differently. This opened something deep in me and allowed gratitude to flow through me."

Maybe you would like to focus on a character-defining moment for a loved one that you witnessed. I find that it is wonderful to become aware of how truly blessed we are as byproducts of the proud moments we enjoy through those we love. As you bring an image of your loved one to your heart, breathe gratitude into that memory.

When I was doing this exercise, I remembered when one of my daughters was in first grade, she came home one day and told me about a girl in her class who had no friends. At lunch, the girl ate by herself. At recess, this same girl was always alone. That day in art class, my daughter's classmate got paint inside her eyes, and it hurt so badly she began to cry. The teacher told the girl to go to the washroom to put water on her face, but my daughter saw that the poor girl couldn't even walk because she was afraid to open her eyes. Nobody else said or did anything to help her, but my daughter asked the teacher if it would be alright for her to help the other child go to the washroom.

My daughter told me how she guided her classmate to wash her face and helped her get her eyes clean. When done, the little girl thanked her and gave her the most amazing smile.

"Mommy," my daughter told me, "Her smile was beautiful. It took up her entire face. I never noticed before that she is pretty when she smiles. We stayed in the washroom for a few minutes talking and guess what, Mommy, she's funny. I felt so bad for her that she has no friends, so I told her I would be her friend. We played after school while we were waiting to get picked up and I had the best time! I really, really like her."

As my daughter excitedly related her story, she began to cry. "I just feel so bad that she was all alone before," she said. "I thought she was strange, but now that I know her, I realize she is amazing."

Wow! Talk about having a proud moment as a mother! The quality of compassion that my daughter exhibited that day brings me incredible pride and joy whenever I think about it. Remembering that moment raises my vibration.

As parents, we dream of how we want our children to turn out, but there are no guarantees about the outcome. We do the best we can to instill in our kids a sense of kindness, empathy, compassion, and care for those who may not be able to help themselves, but at the end of the day, they are their own people. All we can do is teach and support them, then hope for the best.

To listen to my little one tell me her story was a magical moment. I am proud that my daughter saw beyond the "cover of the book" of the shy little girl she originally thought was strange and had the ability to appreciate the essence of that child, who was incredible in her own way.

Today you could choose to think of moments that you've shared with your child when they were little (or now if they are already full-grown) that defined their values and character and express your gratitude for them. As an example, you could say, *"I am grateful that my child has enough compassion to stand up for those in need. I am grateful that my child sees beauty in others."* Whether you are a mom, a dad, or a stepparent, say, *"I am grateful that I am able to witness my child's defining moments."*

The beautiful thing about doing the right thing and feeling the gratitude for it is that the Universe will always compensate you by giving you more of those grateful moments of love, pride, compassion, and joy. Trust me. I am proof that the Universe mirrors back to us more of the very things we feel gratitude for.

Whenever you are ready to complete your FMTG, make sure you close your practice by giving thanks. You could say something like *"I am thankful to the Universe for all my defining moments. I am proud, and I am blessed."*

DAY 1 REFLECTIONS

Use this space to write down any thoughts about your experience with gratitude on Day 1. Remember, recording your insights and emotions will imprint gratefulness on your body and mind.

_____

_____

_____

_____

_____

_____

_____

_____

_____

_____

_____

_____

_____

_____

_____

_____

_____

_____

_____

_____

_____

_____

_____

_____

_____

_____

_____

_____

_____

_____

_____

_____

_____

_____

_____

_____

_____

_____

_____

DAY 2

THE LITTLE THINGS YOUR PARTNER DOES

PURPOSE: *TO GAIN PERSPECTIVE ON THE LITTLE THINGS THAT OFTEN ARE THE BEST THINGS IN LIFE.*

Think of the little things your spouse or partner does for you for which you are grateful. Be mindful and notice these actions. If you are not in a relationship at the moment, focus on the little things that previous partners did. It is the things that are done in the background for us, almost automatically, which can easily go unnoticed and unspoken. Give thanks for those.

Proceed to close your eyes and put your hand over your heart while becoming aware of your breath. Slowly inhale and exhale. Do this for a few seconds. Then think of the gestures of your partner. When you have some in mind, bring those moments to your heart, and feel gratitude for them.

Maybe your partner buys your favorite snacks or flowers without you having to ask. I had a partner who would leave me love notes in surprising and unusual places where I would find them throughout the day. I remember once getting into my car to find a sticky love note on my steering wheel. Another time I was cooking and needed sugar, and guess what? Yes, there was a note there too!

Have you noticed that your meal is plated when you arrive home from work or that there is a cup of coffee ready on the kitchen counter in the morning when you are running late? Perhaps it is the way your beloved reaches for your hand when you are walking or driving together that lets you know you are loved and cared for—or receiving an unsolicited kiss.

Wow, do you feel the gratitude just reading this? As a Gratituder said, "The anxiety relief that I have experienced from this FMTG has improved my quality of life. I am falling so deeply in love with my gorgeous husband again that it is priceless."

There is so much to focus on that leads to feeling so grateful to have someone to love and someone to love you back, right? It is easy to become so distracted by the busyness of our lives that we take each other for granted. I find that concentrating on my gratitude for those things on a weekly basis reconnects me to my partner. It really helps puts things in perspective.

Another Gratituder agreed that FMTG helps her notice her husband's kindness, saying, "I was grateful for this exercise because so much unspoken appreciation came out for both of us. In the nitty-gritty of living life, it can be easily overlooked. We have come a long way with daily gestures that I may have overlooked, and so today, I am grateful for all the loving care and concern he does."

If you have someone to accompany you through life that you truly like and admire, who is also considerate, troubles seem so much more manageable. I love the story one Gratituder in the FMTG course told about his wife. He said that his laundry was a source of disagreement between them because it was never ready when he thought it should be. After some time, he began to do his own laundry; however, he would do it at odd times so he wouldn't be in his wife's way when she was in the laundry room. "Sometimes, the laundry was finished overnight, and I would put it aside to fold after work. I was trying to take care of myself and take a little off my wife's plate. When I came home, I saw that my laundry was folded—which is not a strong skill for me. It was such a little thing for her to do but made a big difference to me. I am so grateful to her. She is awesome in big and little ways."

Although romantic relationships can be the most challenging relationships we have, they can also be the most rewarding. It is all a matter of where you choose to put your focus. People who did this exercise reported being amazed at how many things they found to be grateful for in their partners once they took the time to be mindful of the things their partners actually do.

Are things peachy between you and your partner? Perhaps they are, perhaps they are not—either way, your assignment for Day 2 is to let go of the details of all that is not right in your relationship—at least for the duration of your FMTG practice this morning—and make a concentrated effort to find the good.

Remember what I said before: You attract more of the things that you focus on! So, focus on the positive.

A positive vibrational force is unleashed when you suddenly become aware of how much there is to love and appreciate in your partner. It can evoke a palpable sensation. As another Gratituder points out, "This morning as I realized how lucky I am with a partner that would do anything for our family and me, and how much he loves us, a warm, loving feeling burst open in my chest. This practice showed me how my ego keeps me away from seeing the beautiful life I live."

Once you have completed this exercise, end your practice by giving appreciation by saying something like, *"I am thankful to the Universe for experiencing an abundance of beautiful gestures in my life."*

DAY 2 REFLECTIONS

Use this space to write down any thoughts about your
experience with gratitude on Day 2.

_____

_____

_____

_____

_____

_____

_____

_____

_____

_____

_____

_____

_____

_____

_____

_____

_____

_____

_____

_____

_____

_____

DAY 3

YOUR FRIENDS AND COLLEAGUES

PURPOSE: *TO APPRECIATE THE PEOPLE YOU CHOOSE TO HAVE IN YOUR LIFE.*

Think of all the people in your life who are in it not because they have to be, but because they simply want to be. Think of those who are not bound to you by blood, obligation, or indebtedness, but by choice—your friends.

Think of the uplifting people in your life who have earned your trust and the privilege to accompany you in your times of grief. Those friends who have earned the right to walk with you through your journey. In a beautiful podcast from Brené Brown entitled "The Anatomy of Trust," she recaps a conversation she had when her daughter came home crying, sad about an incident with a friend who she felt broke her trust. Brown demonstrates how she told her daughter that trust is like the marble jar her teacher has in her classroom. Each time the class behaves or does something positive, the teacher adds marbles to the jar. Similarly, if the students do something negative, the teacher pulls marbles out of the jar. When the jar gets full, the class has a great big celebration.

Brown tells her daughter that in life, we have to be selective about who we trust. Like the marble jar, each time a friend does something good, you mentally add a marble to your friendship jar. We share our troubles and sad stories with friends who, over time, have proven time after time that we can trust and rely on them.[1]

This morning, as you do your FMTG ritual, think about your "marble-jar friends." With your eyes closed and a hand over your heart, breathe slowly and deeply. Bring to your heart the image of a friend who is unconditionally available to you, someone who, no matter what you are going through, always seems to be there. Can you see this friend? Breathe love into the image and, for example, say, *"Thank you for your friendship. Thank you for your unwavering love and your commitment to showing up for me whenever I need you."*

Send your friend love. Feel in your heart the appreciation you have for them as you are conscious of all the things that they've done over time to earn "marbles" and say, *"Thank you for your unconditional support and trust."*

Maybe you would like to focus on a friend who makes you laugh. You could say, *"Thank you for the laughter. Thank you for always lighting up my day. No matter what mood I am in before*

I see you, with your amazing humor and outlook on life, you manage to elevate my spirit."

And feel free to use the words *frequency* or *vibration* since you now understand their importance. Say, *"My frequency always rises with your company as we laugh at the silliest of things. Thank you for helping me connect to the lighter side of myself. I am grateful to have you in my life and look forward to many more years of laughter together."*

You may choose to give gratitude to a friend who has mentored you, who has the virtue of listening and giving you sound advice that is uncompromised and unbiased. Bring an image of that friend into your heart and, for example, say, *"Thank you for helping me see that everything has a way of working out. Thank you for teaching me to think out of the box and to consider avenues that I thought didn't exist. Thank you for knowing my weaknesses, yet only focusing on my strengths. Thank you for allowing me to feel safe to open up to you without ever receiving judgment."* Say whatever is true for you. These are just suggestions and only meant to ignite your thought process.

In my own life, I don't have a lot of friends, but the ones I do have are definitely marble-jar friends. My friends are solid and enough for me. I am fortunate that the people I trust, whom I can count on one hand, are the ones who will continue to grow with me, and I am sure they will be the ones with whom I will share the rest of my life. Each of my friends is unique. And each brings something different to my life that makes every relationship special.

As you offer gratitude this morning, picture yourself with the friends you love and see yourself truly enjoying life and experiences together. See yourself as being equally there for them as they are for you and breathe in appreciation for being blessed with connections to friends that make the journey a heck of a lot more enjoyable.

Feel the love and gratitude that you have for the friends who are there for you not just in the good times, but who are your rocks and your anchor when the winds of disappointment and hardship are blowing strong. The next time you are face to face with one of your marble-jar friends after this day, also consider telling your friend directly what he or she means to you.

When you feel you have completed your FMTG for this morning, don't forget to close your practice by expressing your gratitude for all your blessings. You could say something like, *"I am thankful to the Universe for blessing me with friends I can count on."*

DAY 3 REFLECTIONS

Use this space to write down any thoughts about your experience with gratitude on Day 3.

_____

_____

_____

_____

_____

THE GRATITUDE BLUEPRINT

DAY 4

SELF-LOVE AND APPRECIATION

PURPOSE: *TO CONNECT TO THE PERSON WHO MATTERS MOST.*

Today you will dedicate your FMTG to yourself. Yes, you! The person easiest to forget. It is much easier for most of us to appreciate others than to turn inward and give thanks to the person that matters most.

This FMTG session wasn't easy for me. Expressing self-love and appreciation is not something that I thought was important to do. Social programming teaches us that it's more important to put the needs of other people in front of your needs. Growing up, nobody talked about self-love. Perhaps this is why I made so many damaging decisions earlier in my life?

Now there is much more awareness in our culture of the importance of loving ourselves. In fact, it is even part of the lingo kids speak. My daughter (currently thirteen) will often turn to me when I comment on something admiring that she has said about herself and smile before she comments, "What can I say? I love myself."

Wow! At the same age, that concept of self-love didn't register for me.

The best way to think about self-love is to think for a moment like a parent. Most likely, as a parent, you would be careful of your decisions, actions, and choices because of the way they could affect your children. And it would be the same for the advice you give your children, wouldn't you agree? You want only what is best for their wellbeing, and you would most likely always be worrying about how to protect them in the future.

So why don't you do this for yourself?

We often treat ourselves with carelessness and put our needs last. The needs of everyone else come before our own.

Now, don't get me wrong. I am not saying that you shouldn't care about others—not at all. Rather, I am advocating that we care as much for ourselves as we do for others—especially those we love, like our children or partners. I'll take it a step further and say that we cannot take the best care of other people until we first take care of ourselves.

Once you learn to express love and appreciation for yourself, your life will turn around. Why? Because when you learn to love yourself, you will make choices and decisions that are very different than those you made in the past when you were neglecting yourself.

When you love yourself whole, you learn to know your worth, to expect better things from life, and from others, and you will tolerate less nonsense. *Loving yourself whole* means you love all of you—both the good and the imperfections you perceive.

People who cultivate self-appreciation make decisions that are less impulsive because they are mindful and try to anticipate how things they do will impact them in the future. They understand that every choice and decision we make plants a seed that one day bears fruit.

In my opinion, we shouldn't contemplate instant gratification when it comes to decisions that can impact the course of our lives. It's like casting birdseed on the ground because it doesn't last.

I have made many poor decisions in my life. Many times, I let my ego and need for instant gratification get the best of me. This tendency led me to form unhealthy relationships and experience a lot of grief, disappointment, and sickness. It was not until I started to practice FMTG and was able to cultivate the powerful *feeling* of experiencing gratefulness for myself that I was able to design a better life for me and my children. Ultimately, I learned that in order to love someone else fully, I first needed to love myself. To attract the great things that I wished for, I first had to believe that I was worthy of having them. If I wanted to attract better relationships, I needed to fix and cultivate the relationship I had with myself.

It took me a long time to understand that the most important relationship I would ever have is the one I have with myself. I needed that time to get to know who I really was—not on the surface, but authentically. I learned to see beyond the masks of the many versions of myself that I fabricated over the years to fit in. Through the act of giving gratitude each day for the person I was, with all my flaws and qualities, I began to connect with the real me. And once I came to terms with who I was, I also had to be at peace and happy with the person I had found. Expressing gratitude through FMTG helped me.

Only through loving yourself fully can you constructively create yourself as the person you may have always wanted to evolve to be. You can be whoever you want to be. But for you to feel whole, it is necessary to build your life on the foundation of love rather than on a foundation of fear or the desire to please others.

By giving thanks for all that you are and *are not*, you will raise your vibration and attract better experiences and people into your life. If you want to attract people you can trust, then trust yourself. If you want friends who accept you, then accept yourself. If you want a partner to love and accept you as you are, then love and accept yourself first.

Proceed to close your eyes and put your hand over your heart as you breathe deeply and slowly while you feel your heart expand and contract. Then, express gratitude for yourself. Say, *"Thank you for putting up with all the bad decisions I put us through and for still loving me. Thank you for our brave journey, for the way you are able to love, for the way you are able to forgive, and for the ways you have managed to be there for others. I am grateful that you let yourself feel, and that you aren't afraid to let your feelings show. I love how strong you are, even when you think you are not."*

Whatever positive images of yourself come to mind, breathe love into them. Think of the things you often complain about in yourself and turn them around by giving gratitude for what they accomplish on your behalf.

I, for one, complain about my ability to gain weight quickly, especially when on vacation. I guess I let loose and eat more than is good for me when I'm not at home. Afterward, I find myself saying unkind things to myself. It is in such moments of self-criticism that I have to be diligent and aware of what I'm saying and thinking.

In the case of my vacation weight, instead of telling myself that I am fat, I say, *"I am grateful for these few pounds I put on. Although I am not as pleased with the way that my clothing feels, I am grateful because they are a sure sign that I really enjoyed myself while I was away. I am grateful that I enjoyed all the amazing foods, wine, and tastes from other places in the world. I am also grateful that my body responds quickly to changes, and just as quickly as the pounds came, they will fall off once I resume my routine."*

Do you see the difference in how this turn-around gratitude mindset makes us feel?

Loving yourself means being able to accept our perceived imperfections lovingly. Expressing unconditional love during the morning FMTG ritual can help us raise our vibration.

Know that learning to love ourselves is what makes us godly; it's what makes us truly whole.

Remember always to acknowledge your genuine feelings, even negative ones. Don't suppress how you are feeling; instead, weave it into the trajectory of better thinking. Many of my Gratituders who repeated this exercise beyond the five minutes as prescribed here, benefited. Self-love is one of those elements that has multilayers of wounds, and I recommend, to effectively heal these, that you repeat this exercise daily until you feel you have uncovered all the coats of criticism and self-hatred you have put on or said to yourself over the years. Like this Gratituder, who stated, "I have spent most of my life actually hating myself, feeling worthless, dirty, and unworthy of love. And so that's exactly what I attracted. I have spent my whole life destitute of inner peace and self-love, respect, or appreciation of my strengths, talents, and passions. This morning's FMTG on self-love was absolutely amazing! It was exactly what I needed to do. I really appreciate myself and the fact that, against all the odds, I am still alive."

The more things you find to be grateful for about yourself and your behavior, the more reasons you will find to fall in love with yourself—and that's a beautiful thing! When you get to the point of realization, the point of loving and accepting yourself as you genuinely are, you will find internal peace because there will be no more internal wars happening within you. As another of my Gratituders put it, "I think self-love is the most important thing we can do for ourselves. Self-love isn't all bubble baths and buying nice things. Self-love equals self-parenting. It's sometimes saying no when we want to say yes and vice versa. It's having boundaries and maintaining them. It's being vulnerable and strong while being soft. It's accepting that we cannot have the good without the bad, the shadows without the light. Accepting that our path is crooked but beautiful. Some of the hardest things I have done have humbled me beyond belief; whether I am simply moving my limbs or completing a marathon, the feat is a miracle that I created!"

As you end your FMTG, be grateful for a perceived "unlovable" part that lives within you. Say, *"I am thankful to the Universe for all the parts of my being. I love and accept myself as I am."* This could be an incredibly powerful and healing moment for you.

DAY 4 REFLECTIONS

Use this space to write down any thoughts about your experience with gratitude on Day 4.

_____
_____
_____
_____
_____
_____
_____
_____

DAY 5

YOUR CLOSED DOORS

PURPOSE: *TO UNDERSTAND THAT NOT EVERYTHING WE PERCEIVED AS A LOSS IS A LOSS.*

As a little girl, I was taught to be thankful for the closed doors I encountered. I grew up with my great-grandmother telling me, "When the Universe closes one door, somewhere she opens a window." But I sometimes would become impatient and ask, "I've been waiting . . . where is my window?"

Since then, I have learned that the Universe works in her own time, not mine. I've also learned that not getting what I want can be a blessing.

We have to learn to trust that the doors which are closed to us were never meant to be our doors. With certainty, I can tell you that all those opportunities I worked so hard for that did not pan out, all the relationships I fought hard to save that didn't last, and all the other doors I prayed would open for me that stayed closed were immense blessings.

The *Universe*, the term you have heard me use to refer to my divine guidance, has always protected me (even from myself) because she has loved me enough not to let me settle for second best. Consider that the ways of the Universe might work the same way for you. Perhaps that thing that is robbing you of your joy because it is not panning out would not serve your highest good.

None of us can see our entire life trajectory. We aren't aware of the detours, the cliffs, and the switchbacks on the road ahead. We must have faith in the unknown, even if the unknown makes us feel uncomfortable.

I bet that if you make the effort to remember certain things that have not worked out as you wanted, you can easily say, *"Thank goodness."* It is easy to feel upset at the moment, but in hindsight, we can see how the Universe obviously had something greater in store for us.

It is important to be grateful in moments of perceived limitation because, in truth, the Universe doesn't bring us things that limit what she has planned for us. If you feel sad that you are alone because a recent relationship didn't work out, think of it this way: If that person were meant for you, he or she would have stayed. Know that there is someone better for you.

Embrace the closed opportunities because they mean you are closer to finding what is meant for you.

When my daughter tells me that she is sad about losing a friend at school, I direct her to shift her thinking. "Don't think of it as a loss because that friend was never meant to be for you."

The next time you feel distressed by losing someone, consider that their absence may have been devised for your protection. Be grateful that the Universe closes doors by removing people from your path who are not aligned with your highest and greatest good. Sometimes the Universe removes people who would hinder the destiny that is manifesting. As we elevate our frequency, we lose friends and people that no longer resonate with our vibration.

I recently saw a pin on Pinterest that really hit home for me. It read: "I asked God, *'Why are you taking me through troubled waters?'* And God replied, *'Because your enemies can't swim.'*"

Today, let's give thanks for the things and people who leave us because the new can only come when we have let go of the old that no longer serves our highest good. One closed door can and could lead you to a better and happier life that you otherwise would not have. As a Gratituder shared, "My whole life, I felt not good enough to keep because my parents gave me up. My mother was admitted to a mental hospital when she gave birth to me. My father took me to an orphanage. I grew up with a feeling that I was different, that I was not worth keeping, and that I didn't belong. Today I get it. That door that closed to me was of a 'normal' family. But the one that opened led to a life of so much more than what my birth parents could have imagined giving me. I was raised by an amazing woman, and I never wanted for anything."

"I have grieved not having a rightful place within a family . . . making up a story that I somehow wasn't good enough to deserve it. I felt that I was just lucky to have landed where I did after I was 'thrown away.' Today, all that turned around. I can see now that I wasn't thrown away; I was given as a gift to a woman not in a position to have children of her own, who was the best possible mother for me—and that I belonged to her. In a moment today, I went from thinking of myself as something to be thrown away to seeing myself as a gift, from being unworthy to being precious, and from not belonging to being part of this wondrous plan to bring together souls who needed to be together. I just can't begin to say how grateful I am."

Now, it's your turn. Close your eyes and place your hand over your heart. Breathe deeply and slowly. I invite you to change your perspective about something you feel disappointed that you did not get. Instead of lamenting, bring that something into your heart and say, *"Thank you, Universe, for not allowing me to have what I wished for. I trust that you have something better for me. I am grateful that you are creating room in my life for better things to come. I know I cannot see right now what you can see, but I trust you. I am grateful that this closed opportunity means I am on the right track for the right one. I am grateful that this closed door no longer limits what is ahead of my destiny."*

The FMTG system is designed to help you accept what is and to feel gratitude for not receiving even the things you believe you cannot do without. The purpose of FMTG is to have you understand that you can indeed be happy before getting things you desire. When you end your attachment on certain things or people, obstacles dissolve. The *need* is the obstacle obstructing the flow of miracles from entering your life. Whenever you pray for something you *need* to happen, you are telling the Universe that you don't have it and simply giving more life to *the lack*, as opposed to the abundance you desire.

Instead, give gratitude for the delay—that means something. Remember, God's delay is not God's denial. It just means there are other greater plans for you. Getting what you want could limit you, and the Universe loves you too much to have you live a limited life. So, be even more grateful when something you have worked hard to get doesn't come to fruition because it means you are on a divine path.

When you feel you have completed your FMTG, close your practice by expressing your gratitude. You could say, *"I am thankful to the Universe as all things are removed to protect me, and the ones meant for me come to me in perfect timing."*

DAY 5 REFLECTIONS

Use this space to write down any thoughts about your experience with gratitude on Day 5.

_____

_____

_____

_____

DAY 6

YOUR BODY'S INVISIBLE ACTIVITIES

PURPOSE: *TO CONNECT YOU TO YOUR UNPERCEIVED BLESSINGS.*

Today you will focus your FMTG on all that is invisible to you, things that work in the background which you take for granted because you are not aware of the role they play in your daily life. For example, did you know that your body regenerates completely every seven years? Yes, every single cell in your body is reborn again once or more during this span in an effort to keep you alive and vibrant. Are you aware of that?

Did you know your hairs regrow each day to replace those that fall? Can you imagine what would happen if the hundred or so hairs you lose every day were not replaced? Yeah! That's something you can be grateful for.

The next time you climb a staircase, in your mind, express gratitude for your joints and muscles that power your movement. Don't wait until you cannot walk or have issues to appreciate what you have. The fact that we can run, jump, or walk is taken for granted by many of us.

Be grateful for your digestive system, which, without you controlling it, converts the food you eat into the energy you need to operate.

Say thank you to your nervous system, which works like a computer network when it gives your body its instructions.

It's amazing all the things you start to notice and give thanks for that you never did in the past when you do the FMTG practice. As a student of mine states, "I have never done this level of gratitude to the parts of me I don't see. Thank you for helping me expand my gratitude with this lesson. I could do this every day and discover new things in my body to be grateful for."

The intent of today is to cultivate gratitude for your body, which is so sophisticated and intelligent that even when it sleeps, it cooperates with you nonstop to keep you alive. Your body operates night and day, like a tireless biological machine.

Are you aware that your heart miraculously pumps two gallons of blood a minute or over 100,000 gallons a day through your 60,000 miles of blood vessels? Altogether, it beats three billion times in a lifetime, all on its own, with or without you telling it too.[1]

Your eyes function at 100 percent at any given moment without needing to rest. Your eyes are the fastest healing organs in your body. Give thanks for these beautiful organs that allow you to see how beautiful life is if you look around. Eighty percent of our memories are determined by what we see.[2] Roughly 39 million people in the world are blind, and six times as many of us have some kind of vision impairment. If your eyes are healthy, be grateful that through them, you are able to see the smiles of your children and the faces of the people you love. And if you are blind or visually impaired, then be grateful that your other senses were heightened to help you compensate and still touch, feel, and smell the wonders of our world.

Did you know that gratitude can influence the process of cell replication in your body? At the end of every strand of DNA is a "cap" known as a *telomere* that is like the aglet at the end of a shoelace. The length of our telomeres determines our life span. Each time our cells divide, they get shorter until we reach the point that our DNA can no longer be copied properly. This is one of the reasons why we age, and our bodies begin to wither.

Fortunately, we can influence the replication span of our cells through the process of feeling and expressing gratitude. Your practice of FMTG might be able to help you reduce stress, which is known to weaken our body's natural ability to regenerate.

As you can see, there is so much to be thankful for once we become mindful of the invisible things working in the background of our physical bodies to maintain our lives.

With your eyes closed and a hand over your heart, breathe slowly and deeply. Feel your beautiful heart expanding with life with each inhalation while you think of all the different parts of your body that were mentioned above and any others you like. Bring images of those things to your heart as you breathe gratitude for each of them.

See and feel the internal parts of you working perfectly and efficiently as you take none of it for granted. Express gratitude for all your senses, saying, *"Thank you for being able to see, hear, and touch. Thank you for my ability to taste, feel, laugh, and love."*

Say, *"Thank you for my strong immune system, my first line of defense for working harmoniously with my cells to protect me against foreign invaders."*

One technique that helps me is to visualize my immune system as a strong army of soldiers dressed in armor ready for war, producing antibodies—the weapons to fight antigens (terrorists and invaders) that can harm you. Breathe love and gratitude for the role they play in your life and say, *"Thank you for standing on guard to protect me."*

The things we often take for granted are truly things of wonder. As one Gratituder told me, "FMTG taught me that I have been focusing on the wrong things. I've been struggling because I looked to the external world when the internal world has so much to be in awe of. Thank you."

Spending a few minutes in concentrated gratitude for life itself, for all that you have, and for all that you are, could help sustain your life. Your body is wonderful. It is important to give thanks for the small, overlooked things your body does for you because this is the key to unlocking big results in terms of your health and longevity. As a woman who was happily surprised when she tried this FMTG said, "This exercise has made me see things with new eyes and a new heart. This week has taught me to see my body as if for the first time!"

To conclude your FMTG practice and express your appreciation, breathe deeply and slowly, then say, *"I am thankful to the Universe for I am wonderfully and perfectly made. Thank you!"*

DAY 6 REFLECTIONS

Use this space to write down any thoughts about your experience with gratitude on Day 6.

_____

_____

_____

_____

_____

_____

_____

_____

_____

_____

_____

_____

_____

WALEUSKA LAZO

_____

_____

_____

_____

_____

_____

_____

_____

_____

_____

_____

_____

_____

_____

_____

_____

_____

_____

_____

_____

_____

_____

_____

_____

_____

_____

_____

DAY 7

YOUR MORTALITY

PURPOSE: *TO BECOME MINDFUL OF THE GIFT OF EVERY MOMENT.*

One of the most difficult things for any of us is to come to terms with the fact that we will die one day. It scares us. The moment my friends hear me say that we will die someday, I am often asked to change the direction of our conversation. Most people are in denial about dying. Yes, people know they will die one day, but they do not want to think about it. I used to be like them. I was terribly afraid of death—but not anymore. I've come to realize that it was not dying that I was afraid of; it was the prospect of missing my loved ones.

Coming to terms with our mortality is a good thing because it makes us more appreciative of the time we have here. We are on borrowed time and must live life to the fullest and not postpone living for tomorrow.

Today, your assignment is to spend your waking hours in profound admiration for life and all that it brings you. This includes your children, your partner, or whomever you love, because exchanging love is the best reason for living. Don't waste today sweating the small stuff, or even the big stuff, because none of it will matter in the end. All that will matter is who you loved, who you served, and whose life you made better because you were there for them. Truly, that is all that matters.

When we become conscious of living on borrowed time, our perspective towards life and events changes. Think about it for a second. If you knew that today was going to be your last day on earth, how would you spend it? What would you do? What would you say to those you love? I bet you wouldn't waste time being upset or worried about things. I bet you would embrace life wholeheartedly, and you would try to live it to the fullest.

Similarly, if a loved one was on his or her last day, how would you treat them? My hope for you is that, on this day, you will live assuming it could be your last day.

Coming to terms with my ultimate death has made me more focused on the present and helped me enjoy the little things in my life. So, I invite you to connect to this inevitable truth and embrace it, rather than fearing or rejecting it.

With eyes closed and your hand over your heart, breathe life-giving oxygen into your lungs, and say, *"I am grateful that today I was granted the gift to be alive one more day."*

Again, breathe deeply and slowly while sending love to life itself, and as you do, say, *"I am grateful for the opportunity to see the light of day again. I know being alive is a privilege, so I won't waste any part of this day. I won't let this day go in vain. I will get up from this bed with a renewed sense of bliss, and I won't allow my troubles to overshadow the miracle of the day."*

After doing the Day 7 FMTG practice, one Gratituder said, "How you describe being given another day as a privilege hit home. The way I understand it is that I'm being given an opportunity of another day, this day, today. I feel I have an obligation, a duty: It cannot go wasted because it has been denied to others. I have to appreciate and make good use of my time, my decisions, my thoughts, my actions. The FMTG shifted my perspective. Thank you."

There is a famous line from Native American history that was spoken by Chief Oglala Lakota Low Dog before the Battle Little Bighorn: "This is a good day to die." It is not that he wished for his people to die, not at all. What he meant was that they would do what was necessary. I interpret it also to mean that he lived without regrets, without leaving anything he could have done today for tomorrow. He did not focus on the things he lacked. He lived for the moment. He loved and embraced more, spoke all that was unspoken, and did not take resentment or anger to his grave. We need to live life in this way. For me, it is a reminder for us to live each of our days bravely and to the fullest.

I really admire the attitude of going into a battle with no holds barred. And, yes, there are days when I feel this way, and I say it out loud to myself. *"Today would be a great day to die."*

A Gratituder said, "Accepting our mortality can be a difficult thing. I am grateful to FMTG for changing my perspective. I was afraid but feel differently after this morning's meditation. I shall embrace each day as it comes with joy and love. I will be the best that I can be and serve others with humility. I will love life and look forward to this being a good day to die."

While you lie there in your bed this morning, fall in love with your life. As you go about your day, remember to live the day as if it were your last. As one of my students reminded me, "The only way to beat death is to LIVE, to really live." Love all you can, kiss those you love for no reason, tell someone you love them, embrace the work you do, take notice of our beautiful planet and nature, and I hope that at the end of the day when you close your eyes again, you can say to yourself, *"Boy, today would have been a great day to die."*

DAY 7 REFLECTIONS

Use this space to write down any thoughts about your experience with gratitude on Day 7.

_____

_____

_____

_____

THE GRATITUDE BLUEPRINT

WEEK THREE

*"WE HEAL TO THE DEGREE THAT
WE BELIEVE WE ARE HEALED."* [1]

— GREGG BRADEN

Welcome to Week Three! Congratulations on coming this far. I hope you have started to feel the benefits of your FMTG practice and feel excited about starting another week of giving gratitude. Last week, you learned about the importance of energy and the role that different frequencies play in your life. Some Gratituders report being more in sync with everything in their lives by the end of Week Two. They express a noticeable calming of their usual reactiveness and a heightened awareness of negative thought processes. Some Gratituders also notice that people around are kinder to them.

Clearly, as they raise their vibrations, they begin to attract kinder and gentler things into their lives. One of my Gratituders told me, "I have noticed that I seem to be getting free gifts in shops and businesses without asking! I've also received a lot of extra hugs from people in all sorts of random situations. I'm convinced I have a 'blessing bubble' around me, and people react to the attitude of gratitude!"

Another Gratituder reported, "I knew this was going to be a beautiful trip, but never thought that it was going to be so life changing, how each day, you go to the core of something deep inside you. I feel like there is an upsurge of positivity in my life. Starting the day with a focus of gratitude sets the tone for the day, and I find myself being more aware and appreciating more in my life, not only with that day's focus but with the focus from the days that have gone before. I am loving being a part of all this."

During Week Three, your FMTG sessions are going to center on your physical and mental health. For the next seven days, you will explore the role that your emotional frequency plays in sustaining your wellbeing on every level. Your five (or more) minutes of gratitude each morning will help you to release negatively charged energy that is blocking you from experiencing states of peace and joy and interfering with your ability to self-heal.

Every disease that manifests in the body is a result of a preexisting vibrational disharmony. When the body is pushed out of its natural equilibrium for a prolonged period through exposure to stress, guilt, shame, or a variety of poor lifestyle choices, its ability to compensate is overwhelmed, weakening the immune system. This leaves us susceptible to opportunistic infections and malfunctions.

One way to keep your health at an optimum level is to become aware of your body's energy on a regular basis so you can focus on balancing its natural systems and restoring your harmony. You've begun learning how to initiate different states of being at will through implementing your morning FMTG gratitude ritual.

Outside of gratitude, you could explore using techniques like electronic biofeedback, meditation, or sound healing to alter your brainwaves and biology—helping your energy stay appropriately balanced. But none will be any more effective than the very act you have already been doing for the last two weeks.

Yes! Can you believe it? Gratitude helps us stay healthy and strong by the simple fact that it helps change our perspective on life and encourages us to change the frequency of our thoughts for new positive and empowering ones. In many cases, it can even heal chronic illnesses.

Larry Dossey, M.D., a pioneering physician who has studied the power of belief and prayer to heal for decades, has found that people who follow a spiritual or religious path on average live seven to thirteen years longer than people who don't. Dossey proved that engaging in a gratitude practice results in people having a lower incidence of heart disease, cancer, and other major diseases.[2]

Other scientists studying the effects of gratitude and meditation found that when you exercise the act of concentrated and profound gratitude while engaging your heart (as you have been doing), your brain enters a gamma state. Gamma brainwaves (30–80 Hz.) are associated with periods of peak concentration and feelings of blessings and compassion, such as those that monks and nuns experience when in prayer.

When our hearts are feeling love, especially self-love and gratitude for elements of our lives, this is the brain entering a gamma state. This gamma state triggers roughly 1,300 powerful biochemical reactions in our bodies. Among other things, the gamma state increases our immune response and releases antiaging hormones and other substances necessary for the body to heal.[3]

Isn't this amazing? As you give gratitude for what you have, you heal your body, become smarter (due to your increased focus), and feel younger! But in order to experience these benefits and increase your lifespan and health, you must address the things that are blocking your body from healing. As a student of FMTG pointed out, "I knew that this FMTG was the right thing for me to do. Only when we peel back layers of subconscious blockage and connect the heart with the mind will healing occur."

In practicing gratitude for several years, I've discovered that all the willingness in the world to stay positive is not enough to heal a health issue if you don't also address any factor that contributed to the creation of the illness or imbalance. Failing to look at the root causes of their sickness is why people sometimes get better for a while and then, a few years later, get sick again. The illness comes back because they revert to their old unhealthy habits.

Imagine you use a hammer, and each time you use it, it continually pounds on your thumb. You experience a great deal of pain and discomfort. You can remove the pain if you take medication. Once the drug takes effect, you think you are all better and go back to using the hammer, and again, your pain returns.

In the example above, the hammer is the root cause of the pain. The medication masks the pain, but the hammer is still present. Now think about a physical ailment that you have.

What's the "hammer" that is the root cause of your physical ailment?

In the same way that our thoughts and emotions release powerful chemicals that can heal our bodies, thoughts can make us sick by flooding our cells with chemicals that push us out of balance. Becoming aware of just how much time you dedicate to thinking about problems or traumatic events is important. The more energy you assign to anger, fear, resentment, guilt, and shame, the less energy you'll have to dedicate to the creation of a positive, healthy future. Be vigilant and do whatever you can to raise your vibration.

In summary, there is a powerful connection between body, heart, and mind that affects your state of being for better or worse. You can use this body-heart-mind link to heal.

How did I learn to incorporate emotions, thoughts, beliefs, energy, and healing into my FMTG practice, you may ask? By creating illness in my body. I got sick!

Without going into every detail of a painful three-year ordeal, know that I suffered from chronic skin irritation. I went from doctor to doctor, specialist to specialist, undergoing multiple tests for every conceivable virus, bacteria, and infection known to medicine. I was prescribed dozens of medications, including antibiotics and steroids, that affected my mood and weight and had other terrible side effects. The cause of my condition was a mystery. No diagnosis was conclusive. According to medical science, there was no cure. No relief.

I felt like an experimental guinea pig in a laboratory. Or, like my doctors were throwing darts at a target in the dark, giving me all they could think of to see if anything would stick. Whatever illness I had did not register using conventional methods. The doctors could see I had a terrible irritation, yet every test they ran came back clear. The doctors meant well and did their best, but at the end of the day, they told me I would need to find a way to live with my constant discomfort.

That is when my miracle happened. Serendipitously, around that same time, just when I had lost hope of having a normal life, I watched a video of a lecture given by chiropractor Joe Dispenza. He said one powerful sentence that changed my life forever. "If you think logically, a disease is something that occurs inside our bodies. So why would we think we can go outside our bodies to find the cure?"[4] And that was enough for me. Dispenza's idea resonated in my soul, and I understood right then that I, and I alone, had the cure for what ailed me. If my doctors could not do it, then I was going to need to take control of my fate!

I made a powerful decision to heal myself, yet I had no clue where to begin. I made it my full-time job to learn all I could from experts who advocated for the power of self-healing. I was like a sponge. I read books. I went to conferences. I took workshops. And I applied all I was learning to live my life with deep *love* and *devotion*. Having already established an FMTG practice, this information revealed an even deeper level of possibility for what could be accomplished through gratitude.

Healing was not instantaneous for me. I had taken so much medication over such an extended period that my body was overloaded with chemicals and needed to detox. Coupled with my long-term mental and emotional habit of negativity, this state of mind blocked my body's natural ability to heal. But at least I now had hope.

My intuition told me that I now had the explanation that I had needed for so long. Treating the symptoms with medication would not be enough because my real problem was spiritual and psychological, which was why the many treatments I'd tried had failed me. I sensed that I needed to go within myself to find the source. I needed to revisit my past. I knew that my journey required me to set down the heavy emotional burdens of grief, anger, and deprivation that I was carrying. Only when the negative was removed, I would be able to reverse the process of my disease.

The bottom line is that I took responsibility for the life I created. No excuses. No blaming. I took the reins of my healing. I realized that in order for me to heal, I had to release the emotional scars of my past. I had to forgive myself for my poor decisions and behavior. Also, I saw that I needed to forgive those who hurt me and to stop focusing on the things I lacked.

It was not until I began applying the FMTG ritual to issues related to my skin condition that my health slowly began to turn around. Most days, I was so busy giving thanks for all that I had no time to think about my illness. A month and a half into my FMTG practice, I realized that I had not complained of any pain. The so-called disease disappeared as quickly as it appeared. Since then, I have remained cured through the power of gratitude.

The purpose of the topics in Week Three is to help you review your life and heal your emotional wounds. Over the next seven days, I'll guide you to address the things that are stressing you, which prevent you from being in the flow of life. When you address your emotional wounds with thankfulness, you will be amazed at the results.

A fellow Gratituder writes, "I am in awe of this work and the new possibilities that have come from doing this daily practice. My heart is definitely opening, and my generosity towards situations where I felt like a victim is quite remarkable. I am also aware of how often my brain wants to go to problems and how I quickly replace those thoughts with either an offer of gratitude or a statement thanking the thought for highlighting an issue which I give permission to deal with at an appropriate time. The other thing I am aware of is more moments of true presence and wanting to offer generous thoughts to others who are struggling rather than judging them."

Don't be surprised if you find Week Three the most challenging and emotional of all the weeks. Week Three is intense and powerful. You will shed tears, and you will be shaken to your core and triggered as painful events stored in your subconscious finally surface. Don't be scared. This is part of the process. Many Gratituders refer to Week Three as *being inside the eye of the storm.* But as with any storm, there's a rainbow waiting for you on the other side. As other Gratituders did, you may be wondering why do we have to review old traumas? Wouldn't it be more productive just to move forward and focus on the future? After all, the past is the past, right?

Good question!

I was one of those people who asked those questions. I was also one of those people who spent ten years in therapy and marriage counseling. Nothing changed.

Let me explain.

The reason why you must go into your past is that you can't build a future with the same tools you used to make the decisions that led you here. Think of it this way. What got you "here" with all of your pain and disappointments, can't take you "there." You cannot build a present with the same circumstances and habits that led you to the painful parts of your life that you are now trying to forget. We cannot sail to our new destination while we are still anchored to the port. Just because you think you have put your past behind you, does not mean you are freed from it. Trust me. I was carrying that anchor with me everywhere I went: every relationship, my work, and so forth. In order to sail into your future, you must first peel layer after layer and heal each part of your past. Stuffing your past down or pushing it under the rug in the hopes that if you can't see it, maybe it is not there—that's an illusion.

We must first face our traumas, every childhood conditioning, and every societal programming, and through the act of grateful acknowledgment, unwrap it. With acts of compassion and forgiveness, we can heal every layer in our past. Let me clear, the strategy behind FMTG is NOT to relive the event but to face it so you can change the energy you attached to it. Only then can you be free and move forward in your life.

Have doubts? Try it. You have nothing to lose and everything to gain. Invest time into breaking the chains that tie you through compassion, forgiveness, and love. Only then can you release the blocks that cover your soul. As a Gratituder reported, "Week Three was the most challenging for me. Looking back, I realized how deep each day took me. When I thought I knew myself, new revelations would pop up. Some emphasized the me I knew, and some showed me the secrets I was hiding."

For healing to occur, three elements of the FMTG practice are essential: taking responsibility for your past, releasing emotional charges associated with the past (usually regret, shame, and guilt), and forgiveness, both of others and of yourself. Everything that I ask you to do in Week Three is the same as what I did to cure my illness and improve my life.

Are you ready to heal? Turn the page, and let's do it!

DAY 1

HEALING YOUR PAST

PURPOSE: *TO HEAL WOUNDS FROM THE PAST.*

In order to create a better life, you have to be willing to let go of everything that limits you. You must make space for the new to find you.

All of us have been hurt at one time or another, and many painful experiences leave scars on our souls and psyches. Emotions associated with old trauma can get stored in the tissues of our bodies too, where they continue to affect our physical, mental, and emotional wellbeing. Over time, these trapped emotions can lead to disease because they interfere with the body's natural ability to heal.[1]

Today, I invite you to let go of any emotional baggage you've been consciously or unconsciously carrying with you from the past. Close your eyes, put your hand over your heart, begin to breathe deeply and slowly, and then say, *"Today, I am grateful to be releasing the emotional charges that* enslave me to a past that I cannot change. I let go of all the things that have hurt me because they are no longer serving my greatest and highest good."

Tell your body, "We are free now. What happened will not repeat. It cannot hurt us anymore; we are safe now. It is time to heal." Whatever hurtful issues and experiences have occurred, whatever memories of people you have that bring you pain, bring these images to your heart, and acknowledge how you feel, don't hide from your emotions. Give yourself permission to bring them forward. You are safe now. Don't shame or judge yourself for feeling them. Acknowledge the experiences you've had because they have been a part of your life.

As you look at specific events one by one, say, "I release you. I am grateful that you touched my life even if it was for the simple reason of showing that I can transcend difficulties. I'm grateful that this event has shown me that I am strong and resilient. Thank you for showing me that I can overcome you, as today I choose no longer to recall or relive this event. I am free!"

On Day 1, you are going to change the direction and raise your energy by honoring your past and then letting it go. If you have an "addiction" to resentment or anger, fear, and bitterness, your FMTG session today will help you to write a new "software program" into your subconscious mind that changes the flow to more positive emotions. You do this by expressing acceptance and gratitude for the lessons of your past.

As an example, you could say, "I am grateful to be releasing my attachment to this event/experience/person. Today, I chose to use my energy to create new, more joyful experiences for myself. Now, I take my power back!"

After doing this exercise, a Gratituder said, "Wonderful exercise. Recently I have experienced a battle in resisting thoughts of past faults and misdirection. Grateful for this release method. The letting go phrase is powerful. The respect for the lessons of the past is a great motivator to thrust forward, and I am! Thank you."

Many of my students who did this work were surprised at how much emotional stirring can come up about parts of their past they thought had already healed. This is due to my earlier point about the various dimensions of stored pain and cellular memory. They may have dealt with the issues that were on the surface, but this work allows you to go much deeper into the recesses of your subconscious mind. One said, "I thought I put the painful parts of my childhood behind me but discovered so much more. I would never have explored this further if it weren't for Waleuska and her FMTG process. This provided me with a place where we can explore painful parts of our lives in a safe, nonjudgmental space. I've learned through this course that I am solely responsible for my healing, and I appreciate being able to do that here, in the company of kind caring fellow Gratituders."

Deliberately set an intention to surrender the judgments about the past and preconceived notions you have held onto as to how things needed to be. Resolve to stay open as you move forward and experience the life that is truly meant for you. In baseball, you can't run to home plate unless you are willing to leave second base, so let go and run to your beautiful future. Your future does not have to be rooted in your past experiences; it can be entirely new and different.

As one of my Gratituders said, "I have seen tangible changes in my life because of how this work is changing me. Where I was angry and hateful before, I am compassionate and loving now. I nurture acceptance for things I cannot change and realize the only change possible is within me. I am less judging of others. All in hopes of becoming a new grateful person who changes her world by changing herself. Thank you, Waleuska."

As you get ready to conclude your FMTG for today, finish up by expressing your gratitude. You could say something like *"I am thankful to the Universe for helping me accept my life and trajectory in full. I have no regrets. I set myself free from the negative thoughts and stories that have held me captive. Today I fly free."*

Use your past as a teaching guide, not as a predictor of your future. Is there something you would like to do that you have never done before? Time to do it, don't you think?

DAY 1 REFLECTIONS

Use this space to write down any thoughts about your experience with gratitude on Day 1.

_____

_____

_____

_____

THE GRATITUDE BLUEPRINT

_____
_____
_____
_____
_____
_____
_____
_____
_____
_____
_____
_____
_____
_____
_____
_____
_____
_____
_____
_____
_____
_____
_____
_____
_____
_____
_____

DAY 2

HEALING YOUR INNER CHILD

PURPOSE: *TO HEAL YOUR EARLY CHILDHOOD CONDITIONING.*

Yesterday, you worked on healing your past and giving gratitude for the lessons that it has taught you. Today, you will express gratitude for your wounded inner child. Yes! The child you once were lives on inside of you still—and although you may not realize it, your inner child is running a large part of your adult life. Because the human mind operates like a computer, in that it runs on "programs" (conditioned responses), most of the things that trigger you, that you fear, and that drive you to make the negative life choices you make, all took root during childhood.

All your emotional patterns, including the ways you relate to the world and your perceptions, originate in your belief system. You learned to believe what you believe from your caregivers and environment, starting at a very young age. Some beliefs are helpful. But others are not. Those are the ones that I invite you to address today.

Something in your childhood has conditioned you to react to the world in a certain way that is disadvantageous to you. Maybe you believed you weren't loved enough, or you felt abandoned for some reason. Whatever it is, today, you will give your younger self the acknowledgment, appreciation, and love you deserved and did not receive in your childhood.

We all have a wounded inner child that longs to be loved, heard, seen, and accepted. One Gratituder who took my course explained, "This has shown me how important it is to heal my pain from childhood and to come to peace with my father. It is clear now that much of my unworthiness, neediness, judgments, and closed-heartedness is because I didn't know how to interpret events and the meaning that I made of them. I took to heart many things and made meaning that was perhaps not correct, and consequently, I became awkward and very unconfident."

Are you ready to connect to your inner child and help them heal? With your eyes closed and a hand over your heart, start breathing deeply and slowly while you bring an image of your younger self to your heart. Connect to a memory of a time when you were anywhere from three to nine years of age. See this child clearly sitting next to you. What is the child wearing? How is the child feeling? Once you have established the image of yourself, feel your heart expand with love and gratitude for that little child.

Breathe love into the image and tell your younger self, *"Hi there, it has been a while since we connected. I am sorry I have neglected you, but I am here now, and you are never going to feel alone anymore."* Love that little person and give them all the love you needed as a child.

When I did this exercise myself, I saw my younger self sitting next to me. I kid you not. The vision was vivid. I was in my bed, doing my FMTG, and all of a sudden, I was transported to a sandy beach. I lived on a beach as a little girl, so there is no wonder why I would find my younger self there in my vision. And to this day, a beach is still my happy place.

So, there she was, my younger self, beautiful and fragile with a sad look on her face. Her long, loose curls that shimmered at the touch of the sun's rays. For a moment, I forgot that my younger self was me. I felt an immediate urge to protect her, which is the same protectiveness I feel toward my own children.

Now it's your turn to imagine your younger self next to you. Embrace your younger self and say, *"You are loved, and you make me proud. I am here to tell you that no matter what you've been through, we'll make it through. Together we can overcome our trauma. We are free and strong and have a wonderful life. Don't worry about what others tell you, and don't expend energy on the small stuff. Everything has a way of working itself out. I am so grateful to have you with me and to be able to love and protect you. You never have to fear abandonment anymore. I am here with you."*

Say whatever your younger self needs to hear to heal. Participants who have gone through this exercise report feeling many emotions when their inner child becomes visible to them. As one Gratituder explains, "This FMTG session had me in tears. I started with no preconceptions and hadn't really even thought of where I would meet my inner child again, but I wasn't in the driver's seat. My mind took me where I needed to be. The outwardly social girl was where she often was, alone, climbing on the monkey bars or in a big pipe in the playground that served as my getaway. My parents were always busy, and I was the youngest of seven! I never knew until today that I accepted taking a back seat in my family because of my love for them. Inside I would cry, and I have been doing this all my life despite the smile! Today I told my inner child that I am here to protect her and that I will never allow her to feel less important again. I am amazed and grateful for this experience."

It is important to connect and nurture this younger part of us that the inner child represents because by healing it, we heal the adult in us. Because the Universe matches our energy, unless we heal our wounds, we will reexperience the same patterns everywhere we go.

Part of my conditioning as a child was feeling abandoned. Because I felt that I was not loved enough and was not seen or heard in the ways I yearned for, it is no surprise that I felt the same way as an adult. I had relationships with emotionally unavailable men who lacked the capacity to love and accept me, relationships in which I was ultimately betrayed and abandoned. I tolerated this because that was the feeling to which my subconscious programs had accustomed me.

If you want to attract healthy relationships, it is crucial to address your childhood wounds and release their emotional charges. You can't change these events, but you can heal the emotions you felt in the moments that marked you. FMTG can help you process and resolve your archaic feelings and heal.

I love what one of my Gratituders shared after her experience on Day 2. She said, "To my sweet little girl: I give you the permission to talk, to laugh, to make noise, to make choices, to disobey, to play loud, to be proud of who you are, to be autonomous, to ask for independence and get it, to tell your truth, to argue, to disagree, to choose your friends, to choose a man, to love a man, to be loved, to say what you want to say when you want to say it, to be respected for who you are, and to be loved for whatever you do without risking a loss of love and being betrayed. I acknowledge you as a girl with all your qualities and strengths. You are perfect as you are. I love you all from the beginning and will love you till the end. *Je vous aime et protège!* Thank you so much for this powerful exercise."

During your FMTG session today, think of your younger self and send love to them as you say, *"You are loved. You are enough. You can always count on me. You matter, and you make a difference in my life."* Imagine yourself holding that child in your arms and know that you can always connect to them when you feel the need. Healing your inner child is another exercise that I recommend you repeat as often as you need to. The FMTG opens the doors to what is possible when healing your childhood imprints, but truly requires you to revisit this topic for longer periods of time as healing your childhood conditioning is multilayered. A Gratituder said, "I will do this exercise time and time again as I didn't realize how my inner child has literally affected the older me."

I can't stress enough how important the inner child work is and what it can do for you. If you are committed to transforming the adult in you, the only way to do it is by going to the root of where things began. The work is powerful, and the results are extraordinary when you take the time to soothe, heal, and restore your inner child to wholeness. It is up to you to go back in time and make your inner child feel stronger, safer, and loved.

The testimonies of students who have benefited from this work are countless, and I wish I could have you read them all. Another Gratituder said, "I stood in front of my child. I picked her and carried her away with me. I was the person I had always hoped would come to save me from the abusive environment. I am now the future self of that child who made sure she survived and healed. This was a powerful moment. After the experience, I felt whole and integrated with my child's beauty and essence. I love her. I love me!"

After you have done this inner child work for the first time in the morning, feel free to repeat it again before you go to bed, and you will be surprised how your inner child will eagerly show up in different scenarios longing for healing. Embrace this opportunity with courage and grace.

When you have completed your FMTG for today, close by expressing your gratitude, saying something like, "*I am grateful to the Universe for the ability to nurture and heal my younger self, my conditioning, and freeing the adult in me."*

DAY 2 REFLECTIONS

Use this space to write down any thoughts about your experience with gratitude on Day 2.

_____

_____

_____

_____

_____

_____

_____

_____

_____

_____

_____

_____

_____

_____

_____

_____

_____

_____

_____

_____

DAY 3

HEALING YOUR INTIMATE RELATIONSHIPS

PURPOSE: *TO DEEPEN YOUR APPRECIATION FOR YOUR INTIMATE RELATIONSHIPS.*

The person closest to us is often the person who drives us the craziest. They push our buttons and bring to the surface all the unconscious issues we need to heal and address and have ignored, denied, or repressed—and may not even recognize are there. Intimate relationships shine a flashlight into the deepest recesses of our hidden wounds. It is my hope that you can feel more compassion for those you love when they don't get it right because you understand how normal this can be.

Giving thanks in your FMTG session today for the issues that your partner triggers in you emotionally is intended to help you develop your awareness of areas of your life that require healing. It will also put you in a state of appreciation rather than anger and frustration.

Let's begin.

Close your eyes, put your hand over your heart, and breathe deeply. Think of a situation that triggered you emotionally as you ask yourself, "What is this trying to show me about myself? Why do I get such a charge from what my partner said or did? Is this upsetting me because it reminds me that I am doing something similar to myself?"

Stay in silence for a few minutes and see what message you receive from your heart. Recognize that if you are being triggered regularly by this person, there could be something for you to learn. After doing this session, if you do it whole-heartedly, the next time your partner gets you upset, instead of reacting in a knee-jerk fashion, you may notice that you are more relaxed and open and that answers will emerge.

Be grateful for the mirror that your significant other holds up for you to look at yourself in will give you a new dimension of gratitude for the role this person plays in your life. In the future, if you ask these same questions in your mind in real-time instead of reacting to your partner's behavior and remarks, you feel more compassion and can demonstrate more kindness. As a Gratituder said after the exercise, "This exercise brought an acute awareness of just how much I lived unconsciously, allowing negativity to affect my choices and behaviors in adulthood. I am grateful for those who shared part of their lives with me over the years, and who have ultimately revealed so much to work upon. Thank you."

Gradually, as a result of your ongoing practice of gratitude, as you address and heal your emotional triggers, you will have increased patience, fewer confrontations, and deeper bonds of connection with your significant other. Similarly, when your partner is reacting to you, you will be able to step back and understand that their frustration is not so much about you, but perhaps a mirror you are reflecting for them.

Now, as you still have your eyes closed and hand over your heart, recall a moment when you got upset towards your partner and bring it into your heart. As an example, you could say, *"I am ready to see what needs to be seen. I am ready to heal the parts of me that are screaming for attention. Thank you for mirroring these parts, which need to be addressed and heal".* This can apply not just for things your partner triggers you on, but it can be applied for any person that triggers you for that matter. As one of my Gratituders said, "Today's practice was amazing as it did make me stop and contemplate what I was mirroring to a wonderful extent. So yes, I do now have more compassion for my husband and a clearer realization of aspects in myself that still need work. Thank you."

Once we heal what the "mirror" has shown us, the magnetic pull we feel toward any person who is likely to trigger us on this issue will diminish. It may even entirely disappear.

Healing issues that have risen to the surface of your awareness may bring you closer to your partner, but as you heal mentally and emotionally, you also could begin to feel an urge to move on. Sometimes healing means that our contract with a significant other or other people for that matter has ended. The relationship has served its purpose.

That was the case for me when I began practicing immersion in gratitude with FMTG.

I find it is appropriate to give you an example of an issue that hadn't healed, which was brought to the surface for me by a significant other of mine. I had worked for a few years to mend different areas of my life, feeling really good with the progress of my healing, and then, when I thought I had recovered from most of my issues, I felt good enough to date again.

To make a long story short, the man I was dating had a habit of not eating meals regularly—he would starve himself and eat once a day only. While he ate, he always complained, "We overate. I feel bloated, and I feel fat. We ordered too much food." This happened every time we went out. After a while, I began to get terribly triggered. I would get upset and spiral down. I began to sabotage the relationship by avoiding spending time with him just because I didn't like how he always commented on how fat he felt. But at that moment, I was not aware of the reasons why his behavior bothered me so much.

In truth, if he didn't want to eat, I could have eaten and enjoyed the meal myself. After all, his stomach was not tied to mine. I could have chosen to ignore his silly complaints. Instead, they drove me crazy. The emotional charge I got from my boyfriend's remarks was so strong that I finally began to be more vocal about my annoyance and asked if he always needed to complain and ruin the moment. We would go to wonderful restaurants and ordered great meals and wines only to have him ruin and cheapen the moment with his complaints. I just couldn't take it.

The guilt he exhibited over his eating was destroying the relationship for me. So, I decided to ask myself the right questions.

In one of my FMTG morning meditations, I put my hand over my heart and asked, "Why is this behavior triggering me so much? What is it about me that it is reminding me of?" Right away, an answer popped into my head. My heart spoke!

The heart always knows the answers to our questions instantly because it doesn't have to go through analytical filters as the brain does. My boyfriend's behavior did not bother me because of him. It bothered me because it was triggering my negative judgments of myself. He was shining a light on my painful journey of not eating correctly for years and always feeling disgusted with my body—feelings of shame that I thought I had healed earlier.

Looking into the mirror that my boyfriend was holding up for me, I saw the reflection of feelings I had not come to terms with about my eating habits. I was reminded of how intense my body dysmorphia had been. Each time we went out on a date, his comments and behavior reminded me about my own struggles with self-esteem.

The moment I grasped that this was why I was so upset was a powerful moment because it is impossible to heal anything of which you are unaware. Seeing the gift that he gave me, I felt thankful to him for mirroring what I needed to heal. I now knew what to focus on during subsequent sessions of my FMTG. I decided to throw myself into improving my relationship with food and gave myself unconditional love, compassion, and acceptance around this issue. My ongoing FMTG practice helped me feel full and whole, and I learned not to look for food to fill a void.

In that FMTG session, where I immersed myself in gratitude for my boyfriend, my relief was so intense that tears poured down my cheeks. If I had needed more evidence of how powerful FMTG can be, this was it. I now eat without guilt and with full enjoyment. Trust me. I have the pounds to prove it! I love myself enough to consume the healthiest foods that I can, but my food selections no longer come from a distorted sense of having a flawed body, but from loving myself enough to only eat things that give my body life. I regularly let go and enjoy all I want to eat when I travel or celebrate a holiday without feeling remorse for any pounds I gain. If you've ever struggled with your body image, then you know what a gift my boyfriend gave me by helping me move beyond my issues. This is something you can experience for yourself as well when you do your FMTG today. See where being grateful for your annoyance or frustration with your partner leads you. It could be liberating.

As soon as I addressed my triggered feeling, my attraction for the man I was dating dissipated. It was crazy. In a matter of weeks, I felt no pull towards him, and even though he was a great person, I ended the relationship. On a soul level, the issues he was meant to bring to my attention were gone, and so our relationship had achieved its purpose.

People come into our lives to teach us things we need to learn about ourselves. With FMTG, I shifted the disappointment and judgment I felt towards him and replaced them with gratitude. It was also the practice of my FMTG that allowed me to feel compassion for his pain about his body image. Now I feel sweetly sentimental when I think of the role he played in my life.

As Marianne Williamson says: "We are assigned to people with whom we have the maximum opportunity of soul growth. Relationships are laboratories of the spirit, hospitals of the soul. The place where the wounds we hold are brought up because that is the only place where they can be healed."[1]

When you dedicate your FMTG to your closest relationship, the idea is to use it as a mirror to identify any parts of you that may need healing. Instead of feeling frustration and anger, express your gratefulness. Do your best to be open to the idea that your partner has come to teach you things about yourself that you could not possibly learn on your own. As a Gratituder stated, "After this exercise, I see this so very clearly. Synchronized this experiment is my current laboratory of life. One of the hardest things we can do in life is to see this mirror and accept our part in some outrageous situations. When we begin to understand the situations we previously saw as done to us, are orchestrated from a higher plane for our soul growth, we can see our own smaller behaviors that got us there. I see myself. I don't always like what I see, however, that is perspective of the smaller version of me. As I change the aperture of my view, I am able to see more—and I am free. Thank you, FMTG."

During today's session, try to feel grateful for the lessons your partner inadvertently is teaching you and vice versa. Appreciate the lessons! You may grow closer to your partner, or you may not. Some relationships are here for a lifetime, others for a short while. Regardless of the duration of the bond, when you learn to feel gratitude for all your partner has given you, your life will be filled with love, compassion, and forgiveness. Many of my students share how much they benefit when spending more time on this particular subject and go beyond the introductory five minutes of gratitude. Use this tool as often as you need. You will encounter times when an event comes to your life that you need to take a step back to reflect. Once you have completed the entire four weeks, you can choose which lesson you wish to repeat. Depending on what you are going through in your life, think of your FMTG as your healing tool that is there for you. Always!

When you have completed your FMTG, close your practice by expressing your appreciation. You could say something like, *"I am thankful to the Universe for sending me the person I love to highlight the parts of me that need addressing and healing. Thank you for using those I love for my ultimate good."*

THE GRATITUDE BLUEPRINT

DAY 3 REFLECTIONS

Use this space to write down any thoughts about your
experience with gratitude on Day 3.

_____

_____

_____

_____

_____

_____

_____

_____

_____

_____

_____

_____

_____

_____

_____

_____

_____

_____

_____

_____

_____

_____

_____

_____

_____

_____

_____

_____

_____

_____

_____

_____

_____

_____

_____

_____

_____

_____

_____

_____

_____

_____

_____

_____

_____

_____

_____

_____

DAY 4

FORGIVING OTHERS

PURPOSE: TO DROP ANY EMOTIONAL BAGGAGE OF ANGER AND RESENTMENT YOU ARE CARRYING.

G race comes to us when we finally forgive and let go of the painful events from the past that we cannot change. Forgiveness is not about excusing or accepting the behavior of someone who has hurt you. Forgiveness is about loving yourself enough to let go of grief, resentment, hatred, and pain that are poisoning your spirit.

Something beautiful happens when we decide that we will no longer allow ourselves to be ruled by our memories of experiences and emotions from the past. We receive insights. During your Day 3 FMTG session, your mission is to turn all your hurt, all your shame, all your regret, and all your anger into wisdom and self-knowledge. Focus on what your pain has taught you instead of what it has taken away from you.

Forgiveness is critical for your health because when hurtful images are replayed in your mind over and over, your physiology reexperiences the full impact of the event each time. The brain receives a signal of distress and enters into a fight-or-flight state. If you induce this state for an extended period, your body may even become addicted to the chemistry of your emotions of distress.

Your brain produces chemicals to match your thoughts and emotions. If you are inducing grief, sadness, and anxiety by what you focus on, then your body floods itself with chemicals that sustain these negative emotions. Body-brain interaction is a merry-go-round that is difficult to stop without an intervention such as the FMTG practice. Eventually, symptoms will surface in your body in the form of a disease.

Remember, your body cannot discern that you are having a mental experience when you replay a memory or watch a scary movie. Everything in your body feels as if it is actually living in the moment of a past event when you remember it. Your heart rate increases, your breathing accelerates, your throat tightens, you feel pain, and tears start to flow.

Here's a quick example. Have you watched a movie that you've seen before? Even though you know what happens, chances are your heart still races during intense scenes, or you cry when the character is also going through something sad. Now imagine what you do to your body when you replay painful events in your mind day after day.

Logically, who wants to go through a hurtful event if it could be avoided? Yet we do it all the time. To break the habit of introducing pain to our bodies, we must become vigilant about our emotions and thoughts.

The moment you find the lesson or the purpose of any experience (no matter how painful), the emotional charge from that event is weakened, as is any residual attachment you have to the people involved in it. The energetic bond to that person or event immediately shifts. When you catch yourself replaying an event in your head and interrupt the "movie" consciously and consistently enough, you'll transform your hurt into wisdom.

A fellow Gratituder relates her experience on Day 4. "Beautifully powerful and healing. This exercise was perfect for me. I have caught myself far too often entertaining negative thoughts about a certain situation and loved one. It was time to let them go. This exercise taught me grace and ease and allowed me to see the beings involved in this memory in a different holy light. I am grateful."

Don't be afraid to let go of resentment. Surrender the need for revenge. Surrender your need to hear another person say they are sorry or make amends to you. You can't control what anyone else says or does. That's not your journey; it's theirs. All that's in your power is to choose how you will respond when you think of an experience or person going forward. Are you going to move on with your life, or are you going to stay angry and resentful because you aren't getting the retribution you feel you deserve?

Use the daily FMTG ritual to shift your feelings. The beautiful part about this system is that once you learn the tools, you can use FMTG any time you feel yourself drifting into resentment. I recommend you invest time beyond the initial five minutes on this lesson. You can choose to repeat the lesson and stay with it for a few days or a week until you feel you have addressed each one of your events that need forgiving and continue to the following days. Alternately you can choose to repeat the exercise and meditation at night before going to bed while moving forward with the other days during the morning. The choice is yours.

What I can tell you is that each time you repeat the exercises, your experience is different each time. One of my Gratituders said, "It does not matter how many times I repeat this, each time the experience is different because the timeframe is different. What emerges is different each time. Surprisingly, I see new depths and details and new healing taking place."

If you are feeling ashamed or resentful, let me counsel you as loudly and as clearly as I can to STOP! No person or circumstance is worth your peace and your health. You deserve happiness.

Ready for forgiving?

With your eyes closed and your hand over your heart, breathe deeply and slowly in and out while you bring the image of a person and event that has hurt you to your heart and express gratitude for it. When you have the image, please breathe appreciation into it for what the experience has taught you.

Don't focus on the pain, disappointment, or betrayal, as focusing on those things will only prolong your suffering. Focus on the lesson because this will help you heal and evolve.

Your job with your FMTG today is to find something drawn from a painful experience for which you can feel grateful. As difficult as this may prove to be for you right now, go with it. Just see what image comes up! After doing FMTG for a few years now, I can assure you that you will learn many lessons that you will appreciate. I am a strong believer that every experience presents itself to us to teach us something. But it is up to us to seek the treasure in our experiences.

As crazy as it may sound, I've grown to feel that some of my most painful experiences were not mistakes but preordained. Had these experiences not happened, I would not have known true darkness, and without experiencing darkness, I wouldn't have discovered how much light and power I have inside me—and you wouldn't be reading this book!

What is your wound?

In what darkness, if any, are you caught up? Pick whatever comes to mind first as this is a sign you are ready to heal it right now.

Embrace it. Breathe light into it and say, *"Hello, darkness, I am pleased to introduce you to my light."* Recognize that the light shines through the wounds that crack you open—this, in itself, is something for which to feel grateful.

I love what one of my Gratituders said about this exercise. "This one has been quite astounding for me. There was a dear friend who I was completely reliant on as I was new in the country, and she was all I had. I was offered a position of leadership which she had thought would be given to her. My so-called friend withdrew her friendship as a way to punish me for taking the role. I was devastated, and it affected my ability to connect with other people (particularly women) as my trust and heart had been so wounded.

"It has been four years since this happened, and this whole time, I have been unable to let go of the grudge I felt towards her. Using the FMTG techniques for forgiving myself and others, I had a huge breakthrough for the first time about the fact that it is myself that I haven't been trusting—not her or others, but myself.

"I had a lovely dialogue with my heart today, telling myself how much I can and do trust myself. I realized that no one else can hurt me like that again, as I am fully here for myself now. The next day after this practice, I saw this woman in passing, and I was able to have a relaxed connection with her and put closure to the past. I left the encounter feeling relieved from the burden I had carried all these years. Life is opening up and unfolding just as it's meant to, and I love it."

Life is about the choices we make. Only you can make a choice to embrace your pain and find what it has taught you so you may evolve—only you.

Use today's ritual to change your perspective. Perhaps thinking of an ordeal you've survived, ask, *"What is something I have learned from this? What qualities and strengths have surfaced as a consequence of it that I didn't know I had? What* has life presented me with that I would have missed had I avoided this situation?"

Let your FMTG imagery guide you. Let whatever surfaces in your soul heal you. You may be surprised at just how much you can actually grow to appreciate and learn from your ordeals going forward. When we choose to see things as preordained by the Universe to help us evolve, everything becomes a blessing.

I believe in soul contracts, agreements made before birth with the souls of others to experience and heal certain things during our lives. I believe there are people who come into our lives deliberately to teach us specific lessons. Some people come to help us, some to love us, some to hurt us—and we do the same for them. I also believe that these significant encounters are designed to help us learn and evolve so we may reach our ultimate destiny.

If this idea resonates with you, surely you can see how you could be appreciative of even the contracts that disrupt your life and break you open. Your gratitude must be inclusive of the souls who choose to be wound inflictors, no?

If you are thinking about a person who wounded you, with your hand over your heart, say, *"I understand that I don't like the pain you inflicted upon me, but I recognize equally the blessings in disguise."* Think about the outcomes that you were able to obtain because of an experience and say, *"I am grateful that this experience taught me to be more aware, patient, and more cautious. I am grateful that this experience has taught me what I don't want in my life."*

Knowing what we don't is as important as knowing what we do want.

Breathe love and gratitude into the image of a person who made you cry and, for example, say, *"Thank you for showing me that I am strong and resilient. Thank you for making me understand how big my capacity to love is; because even though you didn't love me, I loved you. I thank the tears I shed because they were a reflection of my inner strength and humanity because one cannot hurt this much without having loved that much."*

Whatever the circumstance was, say, *"I understand now that our soul contract was for you to come into my life to put a flashlight into all the parts of me that needed healing. I now understand that what you did to me was not a reflection of me; it was about you. It wasn't that I was not good enough or lovable enough. It was that you didn't think you were good enough. You didn't love yourself enough to be able to love another person.*

"I understand that it was your destiny to be my wound-giver, and for that, I have compassion for you. I am grateful that this experience has taught me that I can love, hurt, and forgive. I love myself enough to set myself free. Thank you for teaching me what lies can do to a person, and in so doing, ensure that I never inflict that same pain on anyone else. I am grateful that this has taught me that there is always hope and that things don't end after a painful chapter in my life. I now see I am the author who writes my own story and decide how it is going to end."

When you can learn to feel compassion for the role that a person has played in your life, either good or bad, it helps you to find the forgiveness you need. Have compassion that, for whatever reason, this person chose to be the betrayer in your story. Whether you are Christian or not, the story of Judas is the perfect analogy for the soul contract I am describing.

Judas was loved by Christ. He was someone Christ chose to be His disciple, who also chose to be his wound-giver. As may have been the case for your wound-giver, the betrayal of Christ by Judas was preordained. Judas' actions were necessary because, without them, Jesus could not have fulfilled the prophecy in the scripture related to His death, resurrection, and subsequent salvation of the world. What if every evil act has a divine component attached to it?

Biblical scholar John MacArthur, the pastor of Grace Community Church in Sun Valley, California, writes, "God used the wrath of Judas and through the deed that Judas did, God brought salvation. Judas meant it for evil, but God used it for good."[1]

Instead of staying bitter about the wrongs that were inflicted on you, consider that perhaps there was a master plan. You may not see this plan yet, but by feeling gratitude for it, you may heal the wound. If you believe that something greater and better will come from this hurt and your heart may feel more peaceful, say, "I know that this hurt is not in vain. Something powerful will awaken in me, and I will be a better, stronger person because of it."

As one of my Gratituders said, "I can honestly say that at the end of this, I am so happy to thank my experiences for the lessons they have brought me. Whether pleasant or unpleasant, everything has had a lesson for me if only I take the time to look for it and focus on the opportunities presented by it. How I choose to react to it is totally in my power, and that is my superpower (like all skills, it takes practice). The future is not here, and the past is gone. Therefore, the only thing that really exists is the present, which really is a gift."

Embrace your pain by giving gratitude to all that caused it. When you feel you have completed your FMTG for today, close your practice by expressing your profound gratitude by saying something like *"I am thankful to the Universe for using my grief as a tool to help me evolve. I now understand that the pain, the betrayal, and the loss (whatever it is you experienced) were learning blocks to give me the humility and wisdom to vitalize my precious life. Thank you."*

DAY 4 REFLECTIONS

Use this space to write down any thoughts about your experience with gratitude on Day 4.

_____

_____

_____

_____

_____

_____

_____

_____

THE GRATITUDE BLUEPRINT

DAY 5

FORGIVING YOURSELF

PURPOSE: *TO BREAK FREE OF THE CHAINS OF*
SELF-RECRIMINATION.

Now that you have spent some time offering forgiveness to others, you must also learn to forgive yourself for the mistakes you made. These may include anything that you consciously or unconsciously attracted for not exercising the right judgment or making the correct decision. Examples may include, failing in business, credit card debt, losing a job, a divorce, a car accident, betraying someone, or not being there for a loved one in a time of need. It is time to let go of any shame and guilt that you feel for past actions and things you did intentionally, which hurt people. It's also time to let go of blaming yourself for being the victim of your circumstances—

for not having the ability to anticipate accidents, crimes, and illnesses.

I know you may not want to hear this, but you must take responsibility for everything in your life and stop blaming others for your feelings or state of being. But this does not mean that you have to berate yourself nonstop. You are not an omnipotent god. You are a mere human and must forgive yourself for your actions.

Yes, bad things sometimes happen to good people, and we feel we don't deserve them. However, in the spirit of taking responsibility for your life, remember that we energetically attract everything we experience into our lives.

It is not that you did something willingly to attract a terrible incident. No. It is that your unconscious state of being was vibrating at a frequency that left you exposed to other low-vibration individuals and events that were vibrating at the same frequency. Of course, there are exceptions, but 99 percent of what we face in our lives is consistent with the frequency of our state of being.

Fortunately, for the last eighteen days, you have been practicing the skills you need to raise your frequency to start attracting better things into your life.

Perhaps you didn't know about how we create our lives from the energy we vibrate until I told you. Perhaps you feel like you would have done something differently if you knew. That's OK. Forgive yourself. Guilt has a very low vibration, so please let go of any shame or guilt you feel for making your past choices, and for any ignorance you have ever had. Nobody is perfect, and we are all works in progress.

Forgiving yourself doesn't mean you are letting yourself off the hook for misdeeds. It just means accepting that whatever you have been through, good or bad, happened because it needed to happen and acknowledging for yourself that there was a bigger plan for it. Remember, there is a lesson in everything if we are willing to look for it.

You may not see or understand the plan, but you can have faith and be grateful that you are in a better place now where you are taking responsibility for building the life you want in the future—beginning by expressing gratitude today.

You can expect to feel more peaceful and lighter after today's FMTG practice. A Gratituder expressed her gratitude for today's practice in these words. "This FMTG totally has changed my life. I have experienced nightmares and love blocks. When I came to this FMTG course, I had received three years of professional counseling and done seven months of inner spiritual work, and nothing had shifted my love blocks or healed me. I was sad and couldn't understand why. Now, after this experience of forgiving myself, I smile every day. Life is beautiful, and I'm meeting new people every day who are drawn to me. My life feels like an adventure. I'm so grateful. This has changed my life."

Another Gratituder said, "There are many things I have constantly felt guilty about. Those negative thoughts have been living with me every day. Whenever something happens, a memory or thought would come back to torment me. It is as if the past and the wrong decisions I made were stopping me from living the present. I followed your instructions, Waleuska. I accepted that I am responsible for whatever has happened in my life, and I have forgiven myself. I have embraced the consideration that I did what I could with the knowledge I had. Today is the first day of the rest of my life because I am free of the guilt, and I accept, love, and forgive myself exactly as I am."

With your eyes closed and your hand over your heart, turn your attention inward by focusing on your breathing. As you breathe deeply and calmly, feel your beautiful heart expanding with life. Be gentle on yourself. Today your FMTG is dedicated to loving yourself whole, loving the parts of you that you have fought to accept.

As you breathe in and out of your heart, transform all that guilt and regret into acceptance. Tell yourself, *"It's alright to have failed, to have made mistakes, to have chosen wrongly. What matters is not where I came from, but where I am consciously deciding to go. I forgive myself for actions that I took that were not for my highest and greatest good. I also forgive myself for the pain I've inflicted on others. I accept that I acted in the only ways I knew how to, given my mental state. Today I know better, and I will do better. I love and forgive myself."*

You cannot change the past. Just know that whatever transpired does not define you. It was a snapshot in time, and you don't have to be the person you were anymore. At that moment in time, you were at a vibration that attracted a certain experience, and you now are vibrating at a different frequency. Forgive, love, and accept yourself as you are.

When you feel you have completed your FMTG for the day, end the session by expressing gratitude to the Universe by saying something like, *"I am thankful to the Universe for giving me the compassion to forgive and accept myself. Thank you. I am free!"*

DAY 5 REFLECTIONS

Use this space to write down any thoughts about your experience with gratitude on Day 5.

_____

_____

_____

_____

_____

_____

_____

_____

_____

_____

_____

_____

_____

_____

_____

_____

_____

_____

DAY 6

HEALING YOUR LIMITING BELIEFS

PURPOSE: *TO REMOVE THE PSYCHOLOGICAL BARRIERS THAT STOP YOU FROM BEING, HAVING, AND DOING THINGS THAT BRING YOU JOY AND FULFILLMENT.*

We all have a belief system that we learned at an early age from our parents, teachers, and peers. Belief systems vary from person to person. What is essential to understand is that the power we give to our beliefs affects our lives in every way.

The first thing I want to establish in your mind is that there are no limits to what you can accomplish in your life other than the limits you accept in your mind. To help you understand how you've come to have the beliefs you have, I will try to break things down for you to the best of my ability.

Almost every major belief we have is generated in childhood. Beliefs are formed in response to what we hear others say, do, or try doing ourselves between birth and age nine. Any thought you think and reinforce consistently becomes a *belief*. Once a belief has formed, it becomes a hardwired program in your subconscious mind.

Each of us, at some point in childhood, was told that there was something we could not do, and we accepted this as true. Over time it became a belief. My younger daughter, Emma, was three years old, and I loved buying her the cutest little bikinis. She looked adorable and was unashamed to show her sweet belly. At around the same age, Emma started summer camp. While getting ready for a swim lesson one day, an older girl told her, "You have a big belly." This remark affected Emma and made her self-conscious. The following week, Emma asked to wear a one-piece swimsuit. Without being aware of what had transpired, I told her I had already packed her bag with a bikini, and there was no time to replace it since we would be late. Again, the same girl told my daughter, "You have a big belly." That afternoon Emma came home from camp and asked never to wear a bikini again. She believed that something was wrong with her body, and it took her father and me eight years to rebuild her self-esteem and reverse the limiting belief she had adopted about her body not being beautiful enough to reveal it.

How many of us have developed the belief that something is wrong or impossible for us? What is a belief that has kept you limited? Do you see how beliefs can really limit your options and fulfillment in every area of your existence, from career and finances to relationships and travel—and much more? The great news is that gratitude and your FMTG will be your tool and support system to reverse whatever types of limiting beliefs you have formed.

Limiting beliefs can hinder your ability to thrive. They limit you in one way or another—that's why we call them *limiting*. When my brother was very young and learning to walk, he took his first steps in one room of our house. There he would wobble his way from one side of the room to the other, landing on the edge of a sofa he would hold on to for stability, and then he would immediately turn around and wobble back to the other side of the room. This routine went on for several days, a period in which we noticed that he still crawled everywhere else. When brought to that one room, my brother raised himself to his feet and walked. Outside the room, he fell on his bum. He believed that he could only walk when he was in that one place in the house.

This is a simple example, and, of course, adult beliefs can be complex. My brother's belief limited him to learning to walk in the confines of one room until my parents encouraged him, "Come on, you can do it!" With their support, my brother began toddling around the whole house. He broke free of the limiting belief in what was possible for him.

How about you? Have you broken free from a limiting belief? Would you like to break free of some more today and see where new possibilities may lead you?

Evidence of self-limiting behavior is everywhere around us. Our own hesitancy stops most of us and can sometimes paralyze us and prevent us from trying to do all of the things we really want to do that could bring us greater fulfillment, joy, and prosperity, and the relationships for which we long.

Isn't it amazing how believing something intangible—an idea—can be powerful enough to stop us in our tracks in different areas of our lives? What if we cultivate powerful beliefs that would support us in reaching to attain our dreams and free us from doubt and inhibition, wouldn't that be valuable to do?

The purpose of your FMTG today is to make you aware of the beliefs you have that interfere with your ability to live a life of joy and abundance. Imagine that your life is a garden of fruit trees, and you are an arborist. The good news is that you are holding in your hands a tool, your FMTG practice, which is like a pair of shears with which you can reverse your limitations. Use the FMTG to prune the old beliefs in your mind and make space to sprout new, more empowering ones.

Before you do your Day 6 FMTG practice, what are some limiting beliefs you have that you would like to prune back? Here are some examples of common beliefs to prompt you to fill in the blank. Adapt these statements to suit your personal circumstances.

"It is not possible for me to . . ."

"I am not worthy of . . ."

"I don't deserve to . . ."

"Money corrupts."

"The world is . . . against me [or a scary place, and so on]."

"I always get sick."

"I catch colds easily . . ."

"All relationships end."

"I don't fit in because . . ."

"My father/mother had ___, so I will develop it too."

"Nothing ever works out for me."

"When something good happens, something bad is sure to follow."

"I gain weight easily."

The list of possibilities is endless. Identifying what your limiting beliefs typically are will enable you to catch yourself and interrupt the thought each time you notice yourself having it.

The power of limiting beliefs over us can be dissolved, in my opinion, by practicing four simple steps.

1. Become clear on what your limiting beliefs are and identify if that belief was yours or whether was a belief you adopted from your caregivers.

2. Replace the limiting thought with a positive, more empowering affirmation.

3. Look for evidence in your past and present behavior and performance that will show you how the belief you held was untrue.

4. Feel gratitude for the new empowering thought you are affirming to *be* or *become* as if you already are.

Missing a step in this process won't give you the results you want. You must do all three, but the third is most important because if you fail to *feel* in your body with all your senses the gratitude for what you are trying to create, all you'll be doing is saying empty affirmations. So, I'd like you to think about the things you have not been able to do simply due to a belief, how ideas have prevented you from having the life you were meant to have.

In my opinion, three especially pernicious beliefs are the worst: the "not-enough" beliefs. *"I am not capable enough, good enough, or smart enough to . . ."* —those three often go hand in hand and wreak havoc when they show up.

I have a friend who, to the outside world, appears to be strong. But inside, he is a wounded boy. Like many of us, he suffers at an unconscious level from the *not-enough* beliefs. For the sake of privacy, I will call him Benjie though this is not his real name. Benjie was smart, driven, ambitious, resourceful, resilient, and visionary. In my eyes, he was my hero. My entire life, I wanted to be as good as Benjie.

It is interesting how we see others versus how they view themselves. This hero of mine went through the majority of his life, believing he had to buy people's affection. Why? Because he believed he was not good enough for people to love and accept him for who he was. As a kid, he would give his classmates candy in hopes of being liked. As an adult, he founded a company and surrounded himself with people he deemed smarter than himself, and some of these people took advantage of him. In not believing in himself, Benjie made poor decisions. At one point, Benjie nearly lost his company to a person because Benjie doubted his abilities. The irony is that once this person was removed from Benjie's company, Benjie ended up doing all the things he thought he couldn't do.

I am not saying Benjie should not have tried to surround himself with capable people. What I am saying is that he needed to stop believing that he had to give a piece of himself away and betray himself or his values to be liked and accepted.

Are there any ways in which your beliefs are causing you pain or preventing you from making the best choices and reaching for the things you desire? During today's FMTG practice, you will take control of your mind by identifying beliefs that do not serve your highest good and turning them around to their opposites—and then sending gratitude to those positive beliefs.

For example, instead of saying, *"I am a loser"* (limiting), you could say, *"I am so grateful that I am a doer, I am victorious"* (positive). Be sure to phrase the affirmative statement in the present tense and say it with gratitude and feeling. Scan your memory banks for an instance for which this new replacement belief was true. It can be small.

As you lie in your bed, you can use your FMTG to reverse beliefs you feel are limiting your possibilities with gratitude by saying:

"I'm grateful that I always come out of difficult situations and land on my feet."

"I am grateful that I have people who love and support me."

"I am grateful that no matter what comes my way, I find solutions."

"I am always in the right place and at the right time."

"All things come to me at the perfect time."

"I am always where I need to be."

"I fear nothing as I know I am guided and protected by the Universe."

"*I am thankful that I find opportunities everywhere.*"

"*I am grateful that things come effortlessly to me.*

"*The right people and circumstances always show up to help me achieve my dreams.*"

"*I have a great ability to make money, and I am prosperous in all my endeavors.*"

"*I am never alone; the right partners always show up in my life.*"

"*I am grateful that I enjoy a strong immune system.*"

"*I am grateful that I bounce back easily from any illness.*"

"*I am thankful to enjoy incredible health.*"

"*The more I age, the younger I feel.*"

If not pruned from our minds, our limiting beliefs block our ability to attract and manifest the things we want that bring us joy, contentment, love, and fulfillment. Many Gratituders have asked me why, despite their effort and desire, they don't manifest their dreams. It is due to the blocking beliefs that reside deep in their subconscious minds.

Do you believe that you are not good enough? Not strong enough? Not capable or fortunate enough? Think again! Do you realize the miracle you are? Three hundred million sperm cells made the run to fertilize one of your mother's eggs, and the one that became you was the one who made it. You have already won the biggest race you'll ever run, and you have nothing to prove to anybody. You are resilient and strong. Life wants you, as you are, to be alive and live up to every potential inherent to your genetic code.

If that doesn't tell you something amazing about your will to live, about your resilience, abilities, and strength, and about the value of your uniqueness, then I don't know what will. You wanted this life so much you made it through the odds, and here you are—so don't waste this precious lifetime!

When you replace your limiting beliefs about yourself with feelings and thoughts of gratitude, you ignite the frequency of miracles in your life. By replacing your limiting beliefs with the belief in possibilities, you are changing the frequency of your thoughts, feelings, and being. Anything you wish to experience can be yours, but nothing new will ever come unless you have learned to feel grateful for what you already have. I know I have mentioned this before, but it bears repeating. When you make a decision to give and feel gratitude for the life you have, being grateful for it all, something magical happens. Your mind holds one thought at a time, so while you are busy saying, "Thank you for life, thank you for my abilities and my inner strength," there is no room for the limiting ones.

So, with that in mind, I invite you to close your eyes, place your hand over your heart, and begin to breathe deeply and slowly while you contact your beautiful heart. With every breath you take, feel your heart expand with gratitude for being alive and being yourself, just as you are.

Embracing the astonishing odds involved in your conception can utterly shift your opinion of who you are. You are not a limited being. You are an extraordinary, powerful being.

So far this week, your FMTG has encouraged you to forgive your past, forgive those who have wronged you, and forgive yourself. Gratitude is now as much a part of your daily life as brushing your teeth. It is time for you to embrace a new set of beliefs. You have the will, the intelligence, and the tools to heal your limiting beliefs. Affirm that your potential is immeasurable and unlimited. You are the biggest of miracles. This is how you make the transition from a limited life to an abundant life: by embracing and feeling gratitude for that which you are.

Connect to your heart in a beautiful moment of humbleness in which you can let go of all your expectations and limitations as you allow yourself to experience immense gratitude and love for all you are and have—the fullness in your life rather than any deficiency or absence. There is a beautiful, peaceful feeling available to us that we create when we go inward and connect with ourselves. I am sure you would agree that despite the challenges, life is worth living.

FMTG may have begun as an experiment for you, but it may no longer feel like that to you if you are like others who have gone through the same progression. One Gratituder reported, "FMTG is becoming something that I want and need. I am slowly becoming a new me. This experience on Day 6 felt like I was writing the first chapter of a new life. Thank you." This exercise is one I also recommend you revisit as often as you need. You may need to work on releasing and replacing beliefs a few at a time.

When you feel your FMTG practice is done for the day, complete your practice by expressing your gratitude to the Universe. Say something like, *"I am thankful to the Universe for the miracle that I am. I am grateful that I am wonderfully made.*

I am grateful that I was put in this world on purpose and for a purpose. I am grateful for my abilities and the life that graces me with joy and prosperity. Thank you as I now know I am enough."

Don't stay limited, assuming that which was once true will always be true. It's time to break free. Believe that the world is a wonderful, safe place for you, and the Universe is conspiring to protect you. Believe that you are always where you need to be, that you have the know-how and the strength to break free from the limits of your own creation and go and live your life the way you were meant to live it. And encourage yourself to rise to take on challenges like my parents did for my little brother, saying, "Come on, you can do it." You can!

DAY 6 REFLECTIONS

Use this space to write down any thoughts about your experience with gratitude on Day 6.

_____

_____

_____

_____

_____

_____

_____

_____

DAY 7

HEALING YOUR ILLNESSES

PURPOSE: *TO HEAL YOUR EMOTIONAL AND PHYSICAL ILLNESSES.*

Welcome to the last day of Week Three. When I initially taught the FMTG course, many Gratituders mentioned this was the most important issue for them. On the first day of the course, some asked if they could jump to this topic first. If you skipped ahead to this day, I encourage you to go back to the beginning of Week One. Week One and Week Two help you build the foundation you need to heal your illness. There is a reason for leaving the healing of illness to the last day of Week Three, and it is important that you don't attempt to alter the sequence. From personal experience, I have learned that in order for healing to occur, you must first heal the layers of root issues that made you sick in the first place.

One of the most powerful things we can do to help our bodies heal is releasing all the negative energy we have accumulated throughout our lives. By holding on to our feelings about painful events in the past, we disrupt the harmony in our bodies. That is the reason why in the previous days, I had you focus on gratefulness for different things that have, in great part, contributed to the development of whatever illness it is you are experiencing.

To further your efforts to restore your equilibrium this week, today, you'll send concentrated gratitude to a specific part of your body that needs healing and restoration. Rather than focusing on the disease or illness, you're going to focus solely on giving gratitude for the healing as if it has already taken place.

Whenever you say thank you, it implies that you are saying thank you for something that has already happened. Paying attention to positive results is a crucial element in any healing process—and giving thanks, *as if it is already done*, signals the Universe to send more healing energy to you. Remember, energy flows where our attention goes.

Equally important to understand is that focusing on the illness or discomfort empowers the illness. Instead, you want to empower the healing.

Additional Strategy for FMTG: The Incorporation of Color

Colors are frequencies of light whose vibrations can be useful for healing. Some gifted people see colors in the subtle energy around our bodies. According to one such individual, Inna Segal, who is a pioneer in the field of energy medicine, "Combining color healing with emotional clearing processes is extremely effective.[1] Today, when you are doing your FMTG, I invite you to work with the three colors that have always worked best for me. I will explain the power of each color. The colors you will use are green, blue, and gold. The technique is simple: As you do your FMTG visualization, imagine everything that you see is bathed in colored light.

If you have never done energy work like this before, it may seem a bit strange to you. Please be openminded and play with it. You may be pleasantly surprised.

The Color Green

Green carries the vibration of nature. Green is restorative, and I associate it with oxygen. Having enough oxygen in our bodies is important because cancer cells and microbes cannot thrive in an oxygen-rich environment. Whenever I dedicate my FMTG to the longevity of my cells and organs, I picture every part of me as imbued with a green light. While I visualize my body immersed in this beautiful healing light, I send love to my cells. I also thank the telomerase enzyme in my body for extending the length of my telomeres, the caps on the ends of my chromosomes, to keep me youthful.

As you may recall, telomeres are essential for preserving our cellular structure during duplication, as our telomeres get shorter and shorter, our cells no longer replicate perfectly and our bodies age. So, send your gratitude to your telomeres, engulf your cells with green light, and see the color travel throughout your entire body.

The Color Blue

In my FMTG sessions, I have visualized the color blue successfully. The color blue is soothing, like the feeling you get when you stare up at the great blue sky or the blue water of an ocean. I use blue to soothe inflammation, pain, and irritation. When I was healing my chronic skin irritation, in my gratitude practice, I imagined the affected areas of my skin bathed in blue to receive relief. There are seven layers to the skin. I visualized my red, swollen skin transformed by picturing every layer change from red to light pink, and then visualizing myself bathed in blue light, enjoying my life healed in full and free of every remnant of pain and discomfort.

The Color Gold

Gold can heal any part of your body. It is as powerful as the sun. Whenever I don't feel safe, gold is the color I use to invoke protection. I visualize a bright golden light surrounding me and those I love and wish to protect— including my inner child.

THERE IS A CONSIDERABLE amount of information on colors and energy healing available online. From now on, you can add color to your FMTG ritual whenever you want.

Today, with your eyes closed and a hand over your heart, bring an image of a part of your body that needs healing to your heart. Once you have a clear image of the body part, picture a colored light entering your body and while you breathe deeply, engulf the affected area while you send unconditional love to it. Experiment with green, blue, or gold light (and possibly other colors of light), following your intuition about which will be most helpful to the affected area today.

By sending love to a part of your body that is hurting, you ignite the power of your body to self-heal. How? Because your brain is the most efficient chemist there is. The human body has the capability to create and release powerful chemicals into the bloodstream that carry with them all the necessary properties to heal us. When we focus on sending love to a body part, the mind perceives this love and translates it into fuel for healing.

The body-heart-mind connection is powerful. Everyone is born with mystical powers; we are all powerful beyond our conscious awareness. This means you can heal yourself because you are innately wired to thrive. You have within you all you need to change your body's hormonal imbalances, reverse unhealthy gene expression, and reverse illnesses.

While you have your eyes closed and your hand over your heart during an FMTG session, see yourself behaving in the way you would behave if you were already free of your symptoms.

How would you feel and what would you be doing if you were vibrantly healthy? When you see an image of your healed state, hold on to it and say, *"I am healed. I have within me all that is needed to have a healthy ___* [describe a quality of your healthy state]." For example, if you have a rash, you could say, *"I am healed. I have within me all that is needed to have healthy, supple, clear skin."*

Words have power when combined with emotions and beliefs, especially when *heartfelt feelings* are concentrated by gratitude. If you believe your words, you have enough power to will new circumstances into existence. This is how you will become a magnet for miracles.

During your FMTG, say, as an example, *"I am grateful that my body knows what to do. I am grateful that I am free of pain. I am grateful that my body is a sophisticated machine that regenerates, recalibrates, and produces all the chemicals it needs to sustain life."* Have faith that your body knows how to heal.

Repeat today's practice as often as you want. If you can ignite the feeling of a healed body on a consistent basis, then you will recruit your brain's assistance. The mind responds to the body, and the body cannot discern if an event is happening by thought alone. To the body, every thought is real. Use this practice to encourage your mind to create healing chemicals that will be stronger than the strongest antibiotic or pharmaceutical medication.

Do not deny reality. Just do not give your current condition more energy than it already has taken from you.

The best way to embrace reality is by being grateful for your symptoms. Instead of worrying about the consequences of the condition you have, turn your concerns around, and feel gratitude. The fact that you are feeling symptoms means your beautiful body is working as it should by alerting you to the areas where you need to pay attention. Think of a car that has an alert light that goes on to signal when it needs to be serviced. Our bodies operate in much the same way. When a light on your dashboard signals, you don't panic. You take action to correct the issue to which you're being alerted. Apply the same principle when you start to feel out of balance. Symptoms of pain and discomfort are the language our bodies use to communicate with us. The power of this approach is perfectly expressed by a Gratituder who said, "I absolutely love the new way of looking at the symptoms and how easy it is to get from being a victim into being in control. Thank you for this invaluable gift. This is a turning moment."

In general, the service our bodies need involves reducing stress, anger, abuse, and increasing love and gratitude.

Isn't it amazing how intelligent the human body is? Symptoms are a way it shows us that it loves us. Be happy that it is doing what is supposed to this morning, and say, *"I thank you for sending these symptoms because without them I would not know what I need to address. I am grateful you are working as you should and for showing me what needs change."*

One of my Gratituders told me, "This exercise was very important for me. I hold on to things way too much. I replay past conversations, actions, and decisions and beat myself up over and over. On a physical level, I have a constant ache and tightness on my shoulders and neck. But I suddenly see that after practicing FMTG for a few weeks, I can hardly feel the tension anymore. I feel a sort of lightness in the area as if I can feel my blood flowing more freely there."

FMTG for a Body Part of Your Own Choosing

With your eyes closed and your hand over your heart, focus on an area that you are in need of healing. Place your attention on the symptom or discomfort that you are feeling and name it. As you say what you are feeling in your mind, express gratitude. If it is fever you are battling, thank the fever. You could say, *"I am thankful to my body for this fever manifesting to protect me. Thank you for raising my temperature to help kill any bacteria and pathogens that threaten to infect my body."*

Another example: If you have arthritis, engulf your affected area with a color of your choosing, and in your mind, send that color energy to your affected area while you visualize the area fully healing. Say, *"I am grateful that the inflammation on my _____ is returning to normal. I am grateful that my body restores all my soft tissues with fluid that nourishes and promotes healthy cartilage growth in my joints, for that I am thankful."*

Choose and say whatever it is that is true for you. Find a way to honor the symptoms and to thank, in advance, for your healing as if it has already taken place.

After you look at the physical manifestation of your illness or condition, it's very beneficial to look at the emotional response you're feeling in regard to your illness or condition—whether you have a sprained ankle, a fever, or cancer.

The FMTG's goal is to have you look at any serious illness as a blessing rather than as a "death sentence" because 70 percent of our health issues can be healed or managed by modifying our lifestyle, reducing our stress, elevating the frequency of our emotions, and expressing gratitude.

The relatively new science of epigenetics studies the role of the environment on our genetic expression. The environment includes our thoughts, perceptions, and emotions. The brain responds to all mental activity by releasing chemicals that affect our genes.[2]

If you have a victim mentality, including the belief that your genes control you and, therefore, there is nothing you can do to alter the *hand* that has been given to you, speaking health-wise, use your FMTG practice to turn those beliefs around. The excuse that we have no choice is no longer valid. The opposite has been proven true. You can express your genes differently than other family members—or at least create the mental conditions to reduce or alleviate symptoms to the best degree possible.

If you have a less severe illness, such as a head cold or a broken toe, it may feel like a punishment or an obstacle that is preventing your life from flowing as you want it to flow. I am a strong believer that when you stop asking, "Why is this happening to me?" and come to view yourself as an empowered creator rather than a victim, and you will be able to find the gift in every moment. By practicing gratitude, you can begin to realize that your condition is happening *for you.*

If you stop asking, "Why is this happening to me?" you can address what needs to be addressed and put a flashlight on the things about your life that need be brought into the light.

As an example, I was under a lot of stress and working extreme periods of time on the computer. My right eye had a reoccurring issue with a sty. Every month I had one in spite of the periodic eye care I practiced to cleaning the glands around my lashes. Occasionally, one sty comes up. It's normal. But the frequency of it, the many visits to the ophthalmologist, and the many antibiotics led me to take a step back, and in the act of giving gratitude for the sty, I said, *"Thank you for repeatedly showing up. I understand that this is not a coincidence, in fact this condition manifesting in my eye is trying to tell me something. I am open to finally hearing what it is that I need to address."*

That was a powerful moment. While my hand was on my heart, my heart spoke! I knew intuitively that the sty was my body's way of telling me I needed to slow down. I needed *less doing* and *more being*. Because I had failed to do so, it kept sending me more sties, to the point where I had no choice but to take a long break from being so continually focused and busy. When I thanked my body for doing this "for me" and began to take regular breaks away from the computer, my crazy stretches of recurring sties ended.

Another example as to how things happen *for us* rather than *to us* is when I was feeling enormous distress when my doctors could not assign a diagnosis to my skin condition. The irritation was painful enough, but even more painful was not knowing what it was and why it was happening. Now, looking back, I have come to realize that we don't always have to know the reasons why and I am even grateful for the unknown. Perhaps that was part of the divine plan for me. The gift of not having a diagnosis forced me to look at all aspects of my life. It drove me to work on healing myself emotionally at every level.

If your health issues have you feeling victimized, try expressing your gratitude for whatever you are feeling and thank your body in advance for its healing. In your heart, feel the emotions of having your health restored in full and being free of the things that hurt you. As you do, your body uses all the energy it needs for restoring your health instead of using it to manage your anxiety.

When you feel you have completed your exercise, express your gratitude by closing with something like this, *"I am thankful to the Universe for I am healed emotionally, physically, and mentally."*

Remember that the feeling must be felt ahead of the experience—that is how you attract the outcome from the Universe. If you can have the love and the gratitude for an illness, I believe you have a good chance of not just healing it, but also healing your life.

DAY 7 REFLECTIONS

Use this space to write down any thoughts about your
experience with gratitude on Day 7.

_____

_____

_____

_____

_____

_____

_____

_____

_____

_____

_____

_____

_____

_____

_____

_____

_____

_____

_____

_____

_____

_____

_____

_____

THE GRATITUDE BLUEPRINT

WEEK
FOUR

ALL THINGS YOU FOCUS ON FROM
YOUR HEART WITH CLEAR AND
PURE INTENTION, YOU SHALL
ATTRACT.

Over the past twenty-one days, you have developed a daily habit of immersing yourself in gratitude. This took effort and discipline. If you've been consistent, then there is no doubt in my mind that you've already been experiencing some internal shifts—both minor and major. Most of my Gratituders report that by the end of Week Three, life flows more smoothly. Others report experiencing life-altering results as the daily practice took them to the depths of their souls.

As a coach, I've heard everything from "The topics were tough and emotional. I felt like life kicked my ass" to "Every morning meditation left me with feelings of being blessed. The most challenging ones brought me priceless insights. The soul searching I've done has forced me to step out of my comfort zone. Even though it was uncomfortable, I'm very grateful."

You deserve a lot of credit for staying on the path to recondition your heart and mind throughout all of these FMTG sessions. From first-hand experience, I know that, as we raise our vibrations and move into the light, shadows appear to show us what is unhealed in us—and looking at this darkness inside us can be uncomfortable. That is why Week Four is important for you. I am sincerely grateful for you showing up and being courageous.

The good news is that on the other side of your pain—if you stay the course—you'll experience an incredible side effect of gratefulness, which is a healed life.

Week Four is a special week. Throughout it, you'll be working on the last piece of the FMTG system. It's in Week Four that you learn what everyone wants but doesn't know how to achieve—lasting happiness and inner peace.

During Week Four, from Days 1-3, you'll practice rounding up at a macro level your gratitude for all the emotional pain in your life. As we get ready to go on our final journey, I am here to guide you every day to help you assemble everything we've worked on. Week Four is where you put everything together and feel deep gratitude for all the hurt, grief, loss, pain, illness, and disappointment you have ever faced. You'll explore things that you judge harshly, emotional upsets, and significant turning points.

As always, the minimum time to spend on FMTG is five minutes. It is best done right at the start of the day while you're still lying in bed. But you can do it for longer, and in more frequent sessions, if you choose. This week I want you to be sure to give yourself enough time to immerse yourself deeply. As always, with topics that are robust for you, you can come back and redo them later to go deeper. The benefits of the practice will be worth it.

Let me be clear with you: The most important component to transform your life is feeling grateful for hurtful events.

And before you object, let me stop you. You must trust me on this one! Without this piece, the system won't work for you. Yes, this may sound counterintuitive, but it works. Each day is important, and one builds on the next, so I hope you won't skip a single day.

If you do follow day by day, you'll be able to say words like these: "Week Four has put a spotlight on my core-level pain and brought much new awareness to the surface. I am so grateful to be working this deep and transforming my original pain. I am now stopping my old thought patterns and releasing the emotional charge associated with events and people. This is huge. Thank you."

It is easy to feel grateful when things are going your way, right? It's easy to give thanks when you have all the things you want. But that's not how the Universe works. In order for you to ignite the frequency in yourself so you can radiate high vibrations into all your relationships and every situation you touch, you must first learn to feel grateful for the not-so-good stuff that happens to you.

Know that you are not alone. It happens to all of us! All my Gratituders, who come from over eighty-five countries, have had people and events hurt them. In Week Three, I talked about how people who hurt you are fulfilling a contract at the soul level. The painful events, believe it or not, could have been put into motion for your benefit. It's now time to give thanks and gratitude to the Universe and those people who fulfilled your request at the soul level.

The purpose of FMTG is to teach us acceptance, find and learn the lessons, and let go of the control we think we have in what happens and to surrender to the flow of life.

For many Gratituders, the step of healing pain and judgment may prove to be the most difficult in the whole system—I know it was for me! But I can tell you with certainty that it will transform your life if you give your whole being over to it. When we learn to be grateful for the painful things in our lives, we learn from them, and when we learn from them, we gain infinite wisdom. This transforms us. At this point, we move away from a victim mentality to an empowered one because we begin to take comfort in accepting that things always happen for a purpose.

If you are skeptical about the promises I make, then believe the student who wrote, "After losing my partner three months ago, my life plummeted into the depths of grief and inability to see what benefit his death at forty-nine could ever have. The FMTG experience helped me every morning set myself up for a positive, grateful day for everything my life has given me and taken away. I no longer concentrate on his loss but on all our happy memories, and I have come to the realization that my partner's love for me was all-encompassing—energy that still surrounds me and our home and family. The comfort and strength this gave me are immeasurable."

As you move from believing that things are happening *to you* to believing that things are happening *for you*—specifically, to teach you something you must learn—your brain rewires itself to think differently about the things you don't like. As you change your perspective on events, the world becomes a more collaborative place.

During Week Four, from Days 4–7, I am going to ask you to turn your attention toward the manifestation of the future you hope to experience by visualizing who you want to be, where and how you want to live, your ideal partner and relationships, and the legacy you would like to leave. The purpose of this four-day period is to look forward eagerly and with excitement to the possibilities that await you in the future, such as occasions like a child's graduation, a vacation to an exotic paradise, or meeting the love of your life. Weddings, births, anniversaries, vacations, and other milestones can be manifested as you imagine them with positive feelings.

I don't know about you, but just thinking about doing an FMTG session on happy possibilities fills my heart with joy and hope for the future. For years, I wondered why nothing much happened when I tried various manifestation processes. Only by stumbling upon the FMTG system did my questions get answered about why I was not attracting the things I diligently visualized. In hindsight, with no disrespect to other manifestation systems, I can see that most are missing a few critical components.

Have you ever been to Mexico as a tourist? Perhaps you learned some words in Spanish beforehand to make the trip go smoothly. When you arrived, you were excited to speak with a native Spanish-speaking person. To your disappointment, as soon as you started a conversation, you realized that neither of you fully understood the other. You couldn't string the few vocabulary words you'd learned into meaningful sentences and didn't get the results you hoped for, did you?

Wasn't it frustrating?

Not knowing different verb forms and how to sequence words in a foreign language naturally impedes communication. We can't get by entirely with a few random words or popular phrases, such as *"Una cerveza por favor"* (unless a beer is all we really want).

Between a trip to Mexico to the Universe, what do the two have in common? Well, the same happens when you're in conversation with the Universe. Unless you are prepared to spend the time to learn the language the Universe understands, beyond simple phrases, you end up feeling like a frustrated tourist.

OK, back to the importance of gratitude when working on manifesting the future you want. For a long while, I acted like a tourist visiting and trying to talk to the Universe. Through my readings on the law of attraction, I knew some of the phrases people use to speak to the Universe, but I did not have the fluency with them or know the proper sequence to string them together for the Universe to comprehend my desires.

Then I began to practice FMTG, and a whole new world of possibilities opened to me. I was making requests, and positive outcomes were manifesting seemingly effortlessly.

The same will happen for you.

For the purpose of manifestation, you must communicate with the Universe in the precise language it understands, through *feelings* powered by your *heart*. The great news is that you have already been practicing "speaking" the language of the Universe through your FMTG sessions for the past twenty-four days. But now you will add a few new elements to the routine.

Ready for the instructions?

Instructions for Feeling-Based Manifestation

As usual, close your eyes so you can focus on the internal landscape of your imagination. Put one or both hands over your heart and feel it beating rhythmically inside your chest. Slow and deepen your breathing. Connect with your life force, center, and ground yourself.

Engage Your Senses and Your Heart

Because the mind learns best through imagery, creating vivid mental pictures of the things, people, places, and events you would like to experience will help you attract them. You should engage as many of your senses as you can when you create the mental pictures of what you desire.

Just as it is essential for you to see, hear, taste, touch, and smell your desired experiences, it is also critically important for you to *feel* the emotions related to whatever it is that you are creating. Choose imagery that evokes as rich and full an emotional response as possible. The emotions and feelings of gratitude you generate in your heart for the things you want to create is the language the Universe understands.

Instead of a motionless picture, play a whole movie in your mind of the outcomes you wish wholeheartedly to attract. Just be sure that your intention for the manifestation is pure and heartfelt.

Without understanding the importance of the component of *feeling the manifestation*, I wrote things that I was grateful for in journals, made vision boards, and practiced affirmations for years—and the results? Nothing. It was like being inside my car and wanting to go somewhere but failing to turn the ignition key to start the engine. I was trying to manifest without feelings!

When I added the feeling component to my visualizations, everything changed for me. After practicing this very same sequence you are learning, A student related, "I remember how I manifested my home. I was standing near an open field, and my heart was filled with the desire and feeling of how much I love open spaces. I imagine every aspect of the home and the way I felt about it. It resonated with my soul. A couple of months later, I found the perfect home across the field where homes were located. It was more like the home found me."

Clearly State Your Intentions

Precisely declare what you want. No matter what you wish to create, be as specific as possible because the Universe is literal. Leave nothing open to interpretation.

Honestly, I can't stress this point enough. Sometimes we set an intention and then feel disappointed at the outcome. But if we look back consciously to what we envisioned for ourselves, we may be surprised at how often we got what we asked for *exactly*. Nothing better, nothing worse. I believe that an example here will help you understand how clear you need to be and how literal the Universe can be.

My older daughter, Victoria, set an intention a few years ago to compete at the Royal Winter Fair in Toronto, the city where we live. The Royal Winter Fair is the largest international equestrian competition in the world. It is where Canadian and international breeders, growers, and competitors may be declared champions in their respective divisions. Horseback riders have to qualify to attend.

Victoria worked and trained diligently to qualify. Whenever I asked Victoria what her goal was, she would always respond that her goal was to qualify for the Royal. For a long time, that was all I heard her say, and I knew that this, in itself, would be a huge, very exciting accomplishment.

Closer to the Royal, I heard her say something new. She added to her goal. She started saying she wanted to place. *Placing* in horsemanship means to take a first place or second place trophy.

Now, fast forward to the actual day! Victoria competed among the best riders and won first place in one of the three rounds of competition. She did not win either of the other two rounds. With this outcome, Victoria got what she asked for exactly. She had set her intention to *qualify* for the Royal and to *place*, and that is what she did exactly.

In speaking to Victoria about the outcome the next day, it became clear to me that she had gone into the competition with doubts. Where was the source of her doubts? The Royal was a new experience for her. She did not know what to expect (also given that she was going to be competing against the best equestrians in her division from around the world), she was hesitant to state her true desire—which was to win all three contests—and be disappointed. She had not felt worthy of winning a ribbon in all three competitions, so she cocreated one medal with the Universe and two losses.

Do you see what happened?

After the fact, it became clear to Victoria that she did not set a clear intention to win *all three* of the rounds. Instead, she made her intention general when she said, "I want to place." This is the perfect example of what not to do. When mirroring our energy, the Universe responds to our strongest emotions, and for my daughter, in spite of her desire to do well, her strongest emotions were fear and doubt.

Another thing I must alert you to is that many of the Gratituders in my courses told me how when they did their romantic blueprints they physically described the person they wanted to attract. I caution you not to do that. By describing that you want someone with blue eyes, who is tall and muscular, for example, you are now limiting yourself and the Universe. If the person that is destined for you does not match the description you've given, then you could be passing up on attracting the person meant for you, who does not have blue eyes. So, when it comes to attracting a person, be detailed about the qualities of the experiences you want to have and rely more on the feelings you wish to feel when you are around this person.

Another caveat related to intention setting is that you must refrain at all times from ever asking for things. This is where most people fail to manifest. People always ask for things, and in the *asking for* something, you are telling the Universe that what you desire does not exist. The asking implies that you lack it. The minute you pray or beseech or ask for something means it is absent from your life. You could ask and ask, but nothing happens until you approach the Universe with a feeling of completion. In other words, act and feel *as if* you already have what you desire.

The Universe acts as a mirror, remember? Its gifts to you reflect the things you feel and believe inside. So, if you ask for a partner, or ask for financial stability, health, and so on, you are giving power to the lack, to the loneliness, to the sickness. Instead, you want to ask through the *feeling* and *gratitude* that you already have those things in the present moment.

You can hope and pray all day for financial security, but the Universe interprets this kind of intention and mirror back the feeling of lacking financial security rather than abundance! What you end up getting is more lack.

Instead, use your imagination to evoke the feeling that you already enjoy the things you want in both your body and heart. Praise the healing, the love, the abundance you want as if you've *already* received it. Unless you can connect and feel what it feels like to have your desires ahead of the event, you won't be successful at manifesting and pulling this possibility from the Field.

As an example, I no longer pray for health. I thank the Universe (expressing gratitude) that *I am healed.* I don't ask for money or financial abundance. I thank the Universe that *I am abundant.* The Universe reads the frequency of the energy you emit when you feel you already had your desire met as you already having something or having done something, and then, in turn, mirrors back to you more of the same. Believing and feeling that you already have what you don't have is the very thing that allows desired outcomes to manifest.

The Universe takes things literally, with no judgment. This is why it's important that you let your feelings do the talking for you. *All things you ask for from your heart, with clear and pure intention, you shall attract.*

Lastly, Feel Worthy of Receiving What You Want

While engaging your heart with all your senses, send concentrated gratitude to the mental picture or movie you've devised and remind yourself that you are worthy of receiving the outcome you're asking for.

Your current state of affairs or conditions in the environment may seem like evidence that you can't go (or shouldn't go) after your dreams and be successful—perhaps you lack money to start a dream business, or you can't quit your job immediately because you have dependents, or you don't think you have the talent, the smarts, or the time. Forget all that! Every objection your mind comes up with can be solved.

Your job is to take whatever step you can with what you have at the moment to move you in the direction of the future you just created in your FMTG; anything else is daydreaming. Your thoughts must match your intention, and so do your behavior and actions.

You may not have the resources you need at your disposal at this moment. You may not be able to make the payments for that home you wish to buy right now, but you can welcome it to happen by staying immersed in the vibration of your dream. Over the next coming days, you will generate the vision of the full blueprint for your future life, and then your mind will go to work to find means, opportunities, social connections, and other things that match that blueprint you have given it. Don't get lost in the details of your current situation. Focus on the outcome. Let the Universe, in her perfect way, figure out the details. Let your blueprint and emotions become the magnet that pulls the tools necessary to see your future manifest.

If you go in doubtful, it may not happen, or it may not happen as well as it could. As one Gratituder points out, "Interesting about the deserving part. It was news to me when I first realized how I myself was stopping things from happening because somewhere subconsciously, deep inside of me, there resided an undeserving part of me that was getting in my way. Thanks to FMTG, I learned that I was worthy of receiving good things."

Remember, the law of the Universe is that it reflects back to us what we reveal to it. It, therefore, gives you what you believe you deserve at your subconscious, *feeling* level. It is necessary to *feel* worthy of having that life you are creating.

As it has become the custom, complete, your morning FMTG rituals, by saying thank you to the Universe. But there is one more thing you must do to facilitate your manifestation.

After FMTG Visualization, Take Action

After you have declared your heartfelt desires to the Universe, I invite you to take action—any action. Do what you can with what you have to move towards the attainment of your dreams. Do not use excuses, such as that you don't know how to do it. The "how" of things is not up to you. It is up to the Universe. What stops many people from accomplishing their dreams is that they let their current circumstances dictate their goals.

So, take action to bring you closer each day to your dream, and then surrender your attachment to controlling how it arrives and to the timeline. Your job is stay in the frequency of your dreams. Do what you can and give the Universe time to do what she needs to do too.

Meanwhile, simply stay in the flow of life!

THIS IS GOING to be a big week for you. A Gratituders appreciative of finally learning the language of the Universe said, "Thank you for sharing the Universe's language. I can feel the electromagnetic charge of the Universe in my body when I practiced my FMTG in this manner."

Turn the page whenever you are ready to begin.

DAY 1

SURRENDERING JUDGMENT

PURPOSE: *TO STOP TRYING TO CONTROL THAT WHICH CANNOT BE CONTROLLED.*

Judging things as "bad" or "unwanted" skews the mind to negativity. We judge people. We judge situations. We judge ourselves. Every time we form a judgment or complain, it pollutes our energy field and drains us of energy. Judging is a bad habit that stirs up pain as you end in constant war against the self.

Fortunately, when you surrender a judgment, you also surrender the pain it stirs up inside you. After you stop judging and categorizing things as good or bad, you are more likely to remain neutral and allow the Universe to manifest whatever she wants to manifest for you. When you can finally get to a place of feeling gratitude inside for everything, you make room for higher vibrational experiences. As you let go of judgment, an eminently appreciative you emerges that can roll with the punches. You begin to believe that life is inherently good, and you are inherently protected.

Look for the hidden gift behind the painful experience. I'd like to share an example of how this works from the life of my younger daughter. A close friend was lying and breaking promises to her, betraying her trust. As I was comforting her after she came home from school in tears one day, I reminded her to look for the hidden gift in her pain. While events will come that hurt, finding a lesson in them can ease our suffering.

What was the gift in my daughter's pain? The experience taught her the qualities to look for in a friend. It also helped her identify the qualities she wants to embody as a friend herself. She learned how hurtful being excluded feels, and the power of demonstrating kindness and empathy.

Speaking for myself, when my heart was broken by a lover a few years ago, the intensity of my grief verified that I had the capacity to experience love wholeheartedly. That was the lesson hidden in the sorrow for which I continue to be immensely grateful.

Pain is often our greatest teacher. This is one of the purposes it serves.

To paraphrase the Book of Ecclesiastes: There is a season, a time, and a purpose for everything we do.[1] As Rabbi Steve Leder pointed out in an interview on suffering, the text of the Bible is specific. "It doesn't say there's a reason; it says there's a purpose . . . and that's a big difference."[2] I appreciated this clarification because many things in life seem horrific and senseless. That's why finding purpose in painful events is a touchy subject for many people. Whenever people hear me speak about my views on the purpose of pain, someone is always quick to point out the world's injustices and insist that no gratitude could ever be felt for them. A child's death, a rape, and the Holocaust are often brought up.

Yes, violent and tragic experiences are terribly sad and upsetting. And the intent of your FMTG practice today is not to minimize your feelings or excuse criminals for their wrongdoing. It is to find the hidden treasure in sad and painful events—to allow yourself to remember and to forgive yourself and others so that you can go on with your life.

The nuclear bomb blasts in Hiroshima and Nagasaki, Japan; the Holocaust, the bloodshed in Vietnam, Bosnia, and Cambodia; the 9/11 attacks on New York City and Washington, D.C.; corrupt political regimes around the world that brutalize citizens for selfish gain—it is hard to find reason in any of it. Perhaps the purpose you are seeking in your mind or heart today can be found on the personal level, in recognizing kindnesses shared by individuals to sustain one another as they are going through hell.

Or perhaps you can find purpose in the fact that tragedies lift our collective consciousness and make us more vocal and courageous about standing up against injustice when we see it. Many wonderful treasures of the human spirit can emerge after dark times if we allow ourselves to learn from them.

In one sense, we have a crystal ball! Looking to the past, we can find evidence of the destructive nature of humankind. But we also can find evidence of how to work together to build a better future. Through gratefulness, we can embrace our differences, in our hearts, becoming accepting of different beliefs, gender identities, sexual orientations, religions, and skin tones. Perhaps the *purpose* to be found in events where intolerance was expressed is that from our mistakes, we develop the resilience and intelligence to make better decisions, elect better leaders, build just governments and courts, and hold each other accountable for our actions.

As I've said before, I am not here to change your mind. I don't want to change, fix, or improve you. Those may be things you want to do for yourself. Real transformation can only come when a person's desire to change is greater than their fear of letting go of their emotional attachments, judgments, and perceptions. Here, I am offering you one woman's perspective.

I am conscious that the FMTG system does not bring 100 percent peace and contentment to 100 percent of people who try it. But I am confident that FMTG increases the measure of peace and joy you feel if you learn to look for the positive aspects of different things. You can stay bitter and have a fatalistic view of the world, as many people do, or you can find hope by looking for signs of goodness in humanity. There are people every day doing their part to make this world a safer place. There are programs emerging to clean our oceans, to find more sustainable sources for electricity, to reduce our garbage, to reforest our wilderness, and to save our animal species. These are common people doing the uncommon.

Not everything we perceive as bad is bad, and not everything we perceive as good is good. Things just are what they are. It is our perception of things, the judgment of actions, and the labels and feelings we attach to them that affect us. To heal, you must surrender the judgment. Looking instead for gifts hidden in the circumstances we face is a direct path to an enlightened life.

Once you see how the Universe works for you, you will appreciate how each rock you stumble over on your path makes you stronger. You will be grateful that the friction you experience while moving towards your dreams is polishing your surface. As a pebble is polished in a rushing stream, your so-called challenges help you become the brave, strong person you intend to be.

Gratefulness, at this level, is reassuring and energizing. One Gratituder explains how her responses have changed: "The FMTG has tremendously helped me be more appreciative. When things don't work the way that I expect them to go, I've learned not to jump into negative assumptions immediately. I now believe there's a reason for it to happen, a lesson to be learned."

Today, look at things you have judged as bad and release your criticism of them. These may be past or current experiences. They may be things you judge other people on—for example, politicians, family, or your in-laws—harshly for doing. It could be a terrible historical event affecting large numbers of people, like the COVID-19 pandemic, a tsunami, or climate change. It doesn't matter how personal or universal the thing is that you judge negatively, as negative judgment is always painful. Open your mind to the possibility of ceasing all judging today.

As you get ready to start your FMTG, close your eyes and put your hand over your heart. Breathe deeply into your heart and say, *"I am grateful that I am here today at the perfect time. No matter what has transpired in my life, good or bad, I let go of judgment, guilt, and resentment related to it. I am grateful that no matter what comes my way, I can handle it. I am grateful for my highs and my lows, and instead of complaining, I choose to focus on finding the purpose and lessons in every experience."*

Tell yourself, *"I am thankful that I am at the perfect place at the perfect time. I am thankful that I am financially, mentally, and emotionally where I need to be. I am grateful that the favors of the Universe are always upon me."*

Recall an event you judged from the past. Think of all the things you had to overcome at work. What promotion passed you by, what raise you deserved didn't materialize, what client dropped you, what things have you lost? Whatever it is, say, *I am grateful for this because I know everything in my life happens with the purpose to guide me to my highest good. I understand that this happens not to stop me or hold me back, but to propel me towards something more— something better or greater."*

Recall something you judge from the present that you resent, fear, or complain about frequently, such as credit card debt, taxes, the behavior of your partner or your neighbors, hair loss, wrinkles, diminishing eyesight, and other signs of the aging process. If you're pregnant, you may judge the changes in your body, such as weight gain, swollen ankles, or food cravings. Say: *"Today I release all judgment and accept life as it is and not as I think it should be. I surrender my need to judge my partner as I realize we are different people, and we are both entitled to do and see things in different ways, and my way is not better or worse than my partner's. I accept things are different. I accept my physical changes with grace. I am grateful for my years, as many don't have the privilege to grow old."*

Say whatever is true for you. Be unwavering in your belief that the Universe has your back, and it's a wonderful place to be. As you express gratitude for it being this, your mental filters will open, and you will see how simple life really is.

Let go of the self-criticism. Do you ever get on your own case for laughing too loudly, procrastinating, or being clumsy? Say: *"I love and accept myself as I am."*

Don't you feel incredible relief?

After this exercise, one of my Gratituders said, "This practice has given me a completely new outlook. No situation is bad because I am always looking for the lesson in every situation. I don't feel anyone is 'out to get me' anymore, and I am more accepting of life. I find it amazing because even though nothing has changed in my day-to-day life, I am happier. The FMTG has enriched me. It has expanded me. It has made me find myself and made me be comfortable with what I found."

When you feel you have completed your FMTG practice for today, close the session by expressing your appreciation. Say something like, *"I am thankful to the Universe for allowing me to surrender the judgment that hindered my ability to have peace in my life. I am grateful to accept myself, things, people, and events as they are."* There is a true sense of peace that comes over us when we finally lay to rest our resistance and learn to embrace life for what it is.

DAY 1 REFLECTIONS

Use this space to write down any thoughts about your experience with gratitude on Day 1. Remember, recording your insights and emotions will imprint gratefulness on your body and mind.

_____

_____

_____

_____

_____

_____

_____

_____

_____

THE GRATITUDE BLUEPRINT

WALEUSKA LAZO

DAY 2

FINDING THE GIFT IN YOUR EMOTIONAL PAIN

PURPOSE: *TO GLEAN WISDOM FROM HARDSHIP.*

When Joseph Campbell said, "It is by going down into the abyss that we recover the treasures of life. Where you stumble, there lies your treasure,"[1] I believe he was saying that emotional pain is a valuable part of the human journey.

No matter how spiritual or religious we are, none of us can avoid personal pain altogether. The quicker we accept that pain is the doorway to wisdom, the less resentful we will be when we have painful moments in our own lives. But it is up to us whether or not we are willing to go into the abyss inside ourselves and find the treasures that the pain has to offer us.

In many of the social media groups I participate in, people complain about their hardships, bereavements, divorces, job losses, illness, death of loved ones, and more. Many even say that they are angry and can't believe in a God that allows such things to happen. But in my opinion, hardships have nothing to do with God, and they do not reflect how good or bad a person we are. And how poorly we feel seems to depend on the meaning we give events. There are no class distinctions or exceptions when it comes to human suffering. That's a ticket we all get when we're born. This is where applying what you learned yesterday is important—dropping the judgment around events that often victimize us is one of the keys to lasting happiness and fulfillment.

We are destined to go through periods of grief, where our spirits will be tested, and challenges will need to be overcome because that's what it takes to be alive. However, as Rabbi Steve Leder says, "It is up to you to make sure you don't come out of hell empty handed."[2] How we respond to our trials determines the quality of our lives because, in fact, we only ever develop our strengths full potential if we rise to meet challenges.

Our character is defined by encountering our inner darkness and learning to shine in spite of it. Many examples can be drawn from the COVID-19 pandemic, which is still raging at the time of this writing. There is a lot of darkness in the world right now, with millions of people affected. Yet people have come together to shine their light in spite of their darkness. Of all the countries, Italy was the hardest hit by COVID-19 in Europe. In spite of the lockdown, people helped one another in any way they could. Social connection (hugging, kissing, visiting, talking face to face) is built into the cultural fabric of Italian society. Instead of succumbing to fear and despair, complaining about not being able to go outside to visit their loved ones as they are accustomed, Italians sat on their balconies to talk to neighbors. They played music and instruments and sang songs from their windows and terraces for everyone to hear. Italians did not let the dark overshadow their light. I am grateful for the resilience of the Italians; their actions are an example that all of us can emulate.

Finding a gift in painful experiences is essential for a peaceful life. It's easy to complain about a painful event. In the case of the COVID-19 pandemic, the world we knew was taken away from us. It is in times like this when the human spirit is tested, and we are called as a global family to step up to the plate to show our resilience as a race. There is no denying that the COVID-19 pandemic has taken much such as, the passing of loved ones, not being able to connect to others physically, our freedom of mobility in some respects, and our sense of security. But it has brought awareness and appreciation back to humanity. We have been reminded of the goodness and resilience of our people. This goes to my point that the Universe never takes from us without giving us something in return.

My wish for you as you embark on a grateful existence is to live your life with a sense of curiosity, seek to discover the hidden secrets, the gems of wisdom, the gifts wrapped in dark paper. Remember, everything happens for a purpose.

The COVID-19 pandemic is no different. The coronavirus brought the world to its knees with a *purpose:* so that we may realize that our humanity needs to be bigger than our pride, and our courage needs to be stronger than our fear. The experience showed us that there is no class distinction, no sexual orientation, religion, economic status, or nationality but one single race: the human race.

We are reminded that we are not separate but enticingly connected. What affects one affects us all. We are reminded that we must value our health and our freedom. The world is reminded of how fragile and precious human life is. This virus has given us perspective: We can see that we waste so much energy and life striving to attain things that do not matter matters. Our existence depends not on how much we have or accumulate but on how we can work with one another. Always look for a gift, and you will find one.

Are you ready to do your FMTG? Then, with your eyes closed and your hand over your heart, inhale and exhale. As you breathe, reflect on what truly matters to you. It is not all the shit you have had to endure. It is the fact that you are alive, and there is nothing more beautiful than that. Life is beautiful! Regardless of our trials and tribulations, life is worth living—at least it is for me, and I hope it is for you; otherwise, you would not be investing time and effort in doing this program. Say, *"I am grateful for my every moment, my every experience, my every dark event, and times of trial. I would not be here right now if it had not been for those lessons that now pave the road to the life of my dreams."*

Focus on expressing gratitude for the people who were placed on your path to hurt and disappoint you. Yes, you read that right. Choose to believe that their purpose in coming into your life was to accelerate your spiritual growth. For this reason alone, give them your most profound gratitude.

As you continue to make contact with your beautiful heart, breathe gratitude into all the parts of you who still hurt and acknowledge your wounds as you say, *"I am grateful for healing and releasing my pain. I am grateful for my emotional scars as I can now appreciate, they aren't a mark of my darkness but a mark of my light and brave journey."*

FMTG helps us avoid falling into the trap of bitterness. The healthiest thing you can do for yourself is to allow yourself to embrace the pain and honor it. Don't use this to bypass your pain. Feel it and heal it. When you come to appreciate what the pain has taught you, you become victorious over it. You are no longer defined by your pain, but by your bravery and your ability to transcend the pain. You stop acting like a victim and instead become the victor and architect of your life.

As beautifully said by one of my Gratituders, "Being able to do this practice has given me the courage to explore, release, honor, and appreciate my pain. You have shown me to show up for my own life and to take responsibility for the life I create."

As you get ready to close your FMTG practice, end it by stating your appreciation. For example, you could say, *"I am thankful to the Universe for discovering that behind all the pain, I have incredible strength to accept and heal my life."*

Remember, you have the choice to be free from your emotional pain. Which is why I leave you with the words of psychologist Edith Eva Eger, Ph.D., Holocaust survivor and author of *The Choice:* "We have within us to find meaning in suffering and to be able to turn it into an opportunity to discover something within us that we never thought was possible."[3]

DAY 2 REFLECTIONS

Use this space to write down any thoughts about your experience with gratitude on Day 2.

_____

_____

_____

_____

_____

_____

_____

_____

_____

_____

_____

_____

_____

THE GRATITUDE BLUEPRINT

_____

_____

_____

_____

_____

_____

_____

_____

_____

_____

_____

_____

_____

_____

_____

_____

_____

_____

_____

_____

_____

_____

_____

_____

_____

_____

_____

_____

DAY 3

YOUR CORE MOMENTS

PURPOSE: *TO REALIZE THE RICHNESS AND BEAUTY OF THE DEFINING MOMENTS IN YOUR LIFE.*

Welcome to Day 3. Today you will focus your FMTG practice on appreciation for the core moments of your life. *Core moments* are those that feel central to the meaning you assign to your life. They are moments that indelibly marked you in some way, whether they were good or sad moments. Examples would include moments like a wedding, the birth of a child, or a professional triumph, which bring us joy, as well as moments like deaths, violent attacks, and illness, which bring us sorrow. I invite you, as you look back over the most meaningful memories from your life, to give gratitude for everything that's occurred. It is important to make an inventory of all the moments that mark you as a person so you can better understand and appreciate your journey.

In this FMTG session, you're going to be creating a quilt of significant moments that make up your life story. Imagine for a moment that this quilt of core memories is a treasured heirloom that will be passed on to someone you love, such as a child, a grandchild, best friend, or significant other. Or you may choose to view it as a gift for yourself.

You are going to feel excited when creating this quilt because it symbolizes your life story. You may see that some of the swatches contain sad and happy moments that marked you. Without the sad swatches, you may not have enough appreciation for the good ones. It is alright to have sad moments because they are also a part of your story.

To give you an idea of the kinds of significant moments a life quilt can hold, let me tell you about the ones I used to build my own quilt. I visualized myself making squares from colorful swatches of cloth that included my wedding day, the first time I heard each of my daughters' hearts beating through an ultrasound machine, and then the moments right after their births—hearing their first cries and holding them in my arms whispering, "I'm your mommy," as well as the day my former husband and I signed papers for a bank loan to found our company.

There were sad moments in my quilt too, which I colored in shades of gray, such as the death of my dogs, Charlie and Olive, whom I have missed every day since. The death of my paternal grandmother, who was, in many ways, my mom, as she helped to raise me. Also, signing my divorce papers. That sad moment changed the course of my life. Another core moment I put on my quilt was when my younger daughter, who suffered from selective mutism as a little girl, spoke aloud for the first time in front of others. Wow! Talk about a moment imprinted on my heart! All those pieces of my life became a warm quilt of memories.

As you review these altogether, you are creating a mind movie—a running movie of your life made by your core moments.

Which moments do you choose for your quilt?

Perhaps the moment you want to put on your quilt includes the passing of a parent or another loved one. Often the most meaningful moments in our lives are those that connect us with our mortality.

The moments on your quilt should include memorable, meaningful turning points. For you, a turning point might be the moment of finally landing your dream job or hearing that you earned the desired promotion, the day you decided to move to a new country, raising your hand and swearing your allegiance as a citizen, receiving an award, meeting someone you've long admired, or overcoming an illness.

Ultimately the act of reviewing your core moments like a film gives us deeper insights into the life you've lived so far. The depth of this FMTG experience can bring you appreciation, and possibly pride, for all you have been through and endured. Your quilt is your resilience and the human spirit at its best. The purpose is for you to realize how much good there actually is in your life story. This quilt you are creating with love and compassion, hopefully, serves to focus you on just how much good there actually is in your life.

The purpose of this day is to have you connect to the overall story of your life and feel gratitude for it in its entirety. It can be incredible if you give yourself over to this exercise. As one Gratituder shared, "Never in my wildest dreams did I expect to do such reflection or, with it, such deep and meaningful healing. Doing FMTG day after day is like peeling back the layers of an onion; I am continually peeling the layers leading me to my authentic self."

Let's begin.

Close your eyes and place your hand over your heart. Listen to the sound of your breath. Take a few moments to turn inwards. Now, I invite you to imagine that a large piece of plain white cloth is spread out before you. In your hands, you are holding additional swatches of colored cloth, which are shaped like puzzle pieces. Each of these swatches symbolizes one of your core moments.

As you breathe slowly and deeply, call up images of the significant events that marked you. Bring the core memories, one at a time into your heart, and visualize yourself sewing patches onto the white backing of your quilt. Go slowly. See yourself sew on the first, then the second, then the third, and so on, expressing gratitude for each of the moments you've chosen. As you see your life-quilt take shape, notice how beautiful, diverse, and colorful it is.

Looking back at your life in its totality, for what are you grateful? When you start to see the quilt pieces take shape, do you see how each piece needs the others in order to complete itself? None is separate.

"I love the quilt visualization," a student of mine said. "To see all those pieces coming together—the good, the bad, the pain, the joy, all those feelings—was so beautiful. Yes, there is pain or sorrow or shame in these pieces, but I also see how each next piece could not have come into being without the one before it. I am so grateful for the connectedness, and now I will wrap myself up in this rich mosaic quilt of life."

You may feel grateful when you see how the moments that didn't bring you joy brought you wisdom or that your losses taught you the full measure of your love. The first time I did this FMTG session, I learned that the sad moments were just as necessary for me to become the woman I am today as the joyful ones. In the end, it is all your significant moments combined that shape the quilt that you can now proudly use to "keep you warm."

I love what another of my Gratituders said. "I was humbled by this exercise to review my core moments. I am so fortunate that life has given me plenty of amazing ones. If I'm honest, life has also bestowed my family and me with some pretty stressful and downright challenging moments. But without them, I wouldn't have reached the point where I am now."

"You ask, can I feel grateful? Yes, I am grateful for the grief, as I know it has made me more compassionate. Yes, I am grateful for having to deal with mental health issues in my family, as these have made me less judgmental. Yes, I am grateful for the stress, as it has helped me find inner strength. Good and bad, I'm grateful!"

As you call up all the events in your life and continue to sew them onto your quilt one by one, breathe deeply and feel gratitude. Say, *"I am so grateful for every one of my life events. The beautiful ones brought me joy, and the difficult ones strengthen me. I am grateful for all my swatches that make up my meaningful life."*

Before you conclude your FMTG, see yourself step back and admire your quilt in its totality. Feel blessed for good and not so good events because they shaped the person you are today.

You can come back in the future and add more pieces to your quilt. You can also come back and admire it whenever you want or need to, such as when you are having a bad day. Use it to gain perspective.

When you feel you have completed your FMTG for the day, close your practice today, as always, by expressing your gratitude. Say something like, *"I am thankful to the Universe, for I now see with how blessed I've been in my life. I am hopeful about the future and all the other beautiful things that are yet to come. Thank you."*

DAY 3 REFLECTIONS

Use this space to write down any thoughts about your experience with gratitude on Day 3.

_____

_____

_____

THE GRATITUDE BLUEPRINT

DAY 4

BECOMING THE PERSON
OF YOUR DREAMS

PURPOSE: *TO CREATE YOUR BEST, MOST
AUTHENTIC SELF.*

The purpose of today's FMTG is to remember the
person you truly are and not the one society has made
you believe you are. Everything that you dream that
does not yet exist, you can create—including your dream for
the kind of person you wish to be in the future.

To manifest the version of yourself you wish to become,
you first need to understand that saying you will change
something about yourself, is not enough—especially if you're
strongly attached to the emotional and behavioral patterns
of your current self. It takes great strength from you not to
go back to this old self—let's call it that, even if you're a young
person—because that is familiar to your body. It will crave

the feeling of its habits and try to push you to return to the person you are trying to transform away from because the human body and mind are built for preservation, not change.

So, this will only work if your desire to change is accompanied by enough energy to override your sub-conscious programming. Your job today is to teach your body what it *feels* like to be the person you want to become and show it—through visualization—how your behavior could match that intention.

I myself have done this exercise many times. I love closing my eyes and literally playing out my entire day the way I want it to go as the woman I want to be. I intend to embody warmth, so I envision my kids coming home from school and basking them in the glow of my warm welcome. I picture myself showing my girls how interested I am in their day. I imagine myself playing music in the background in our kitchen while I cook their favorite meal. I see us smiling and laughing out loud as we sit together at the kitchen table to eat while recalling funny stories of my childhood or things we have done together. My goal is to be a person who emanates the energy of happiness. I desire the home I make for my girls to be full of laughter, warmth, safety, and open communication.

I am happy to say that when I originally made decisions about who I was going to be and the environment I was going to create, it took no effort to make the transition in real life. I attribute what I have accomplished as a parent to my FMTG *mental rehearsals*.

My younger daughter always comments about how much she loves being at my house. Although she loves being with her dad in his home, she misses mine when she's away. When I ask why, she says, "The energy here is so peaceful, Mommy. I just love the feeling."

Although she is not able to fully articulate what attracts her to my presence, she describes the energy perfectly when she says, "It is the feeling!" She is responding to the vibration of love, openness, and joy that our household emits.

You can be whomever you set an intention to be. Just focus.

As one of my Gratituders reported, "Yesterday morning, out of the blue, I decided to give up vape/smoking. Although this had been hard for me to do, yesterday I noticed that it was not in any of my future visions of myself, and I no longer needed it." I love this remark because this is precisely what the FMTG is aiming to help you do. It is asking you to create the *new you*—which, in this man's case, was a nonsmoker— and once you have set the intention of who you are going to become, anything that doesn't correspond to that vision will be removed from your life—it may drop away effortlessly.

You can design the person you want to become. Think of yourself as the architect, and your brain is the contractor. When your brain (the contractor) looks for direction, it doesn't have to think separately from your body. Your brain has the blueprint to follow, and it begins to look and find a way to build what you have given it to create.

By stating to the Universe that you already are the person that has the qualities and life you wish to manifest, you will begin to act like that person.

I love the way Joe Dispenza explains this process:

> By mentally rehearsing what you are going to do and who you want to become, your brain doesn't know the difference and if you get caught up in it, you begin to install the neurological hardware in your brain to look like you've already done it. Now the brain is not a record of the past. You are priming your brain for the future and if you keep doing it, the hardware will become the software program. And do you know what that means? You might start acting like a happy person. You installed the circuits.[1]

Before you even realize it for yourself, those around you notice that you are different. That is what happened to many of my students and me. Without realizing, I was imbued with patience, understanding, compassion, all qualities that were formerly foreign to me. I was able to forgive; I was able to reduce drastically the amount of time I stayed in anger or disappointment. My "bounce-back muscle" became stronger each day that I spent in gratitude.

When you give gratitude for the person you wish to become, and you feel yourself be that person, your actions magically match that intention. You will want to protect the person you have created, and you will begin to act, breathe, and live as the embodiment of your future self.

I am not always proud of the things I did in the past. I was selfish and didn't think through enough how my actions affected those around me. I was not as aware of others' emotions and feelings as I would like to have been. Today, when confronted with a situation in which I have to choose between two outcomes, I can still feel a quick pull from my brain saying, "Who cares, just do it; you have in the past, and nobody will find out." I literally can hear chatter in my brain trying to persuade me to behave like my old self.

Sometimes I laugh as I talk back to that voice. My words carry such power of intention and conviction when I tell it, "No, I am not that person anymore."

You see, it does not matter if anyone finds out or not. Only what I do matters. I will know, and that is enough for me. I have spent enough hours with my FMTG creating the person that I am that no pull or chatter can turn me back. I've invested so much into cultivating my best version of myself; I've rehearsed it enough, and I feel proud of who I've consciously chosen to become. I want you to experience that same pride and integrity.

Now that you understand the process let's proceed. With your eyes closed, begin to breathe deeply and slowly, in and out. Place your hand over your heart so that you put your energy and focus on it.

Remember, the combination of having your eyes closed, while breathing slowly and deliberately, reduces the impact of stimuli from outside sources. The less outside stimuli you notice, the more room your brain has to focus on creating the pictures in your head that you'll need to visualize to create the things you want to manifest.

Now, begin *feeling* in your *heart* an intense love, pride, and gratitude for yourself as you picture the person you want to become; but imagine that you already are that person. Whatever your desire is, whatever attributes you wish to cultivate and exhibit on a daily basis, give thanks for already being a person who embodies them. See yourself going about the day and interacting with people as this desired person. You are already compassionate, loving, successful, intuitive, vibrant, and healthy. The more specific you are, the better.

To help you tap into the person you want to be, you could ask yourself questions like, *"Who do I want to be today when I get up out of this bed? What difference do I want to make? How am I going to contribute? Who will I serve? What things do I want to do today?"* Let the answer come to you in the form of a picture, a sound, or a feeling.

If you wish to be joyful, then picture yourself *feeling* joyful, *see* yourself smiling, and *hear* the sound of your laughter. If your goal is to be the kind of person who influences positive changes in the world, then imagine yourself in that situation already accomplishing those things in real-time. Maybe you dream of being an artist but never had the time—make the time to start sculpting or painting. See and feel your canvas taking a life of its own. As you create your beautiful art, you honor the Universe for this gift.

If you wished to become a musician but never had the courage to pursue that dream, start today. See yourself playing an instrument or singing—maybe you *see* yourself on stage as you bow to your audience, or you *hear* them clap and cheer you for a great performance. The more of your senses that you can bring into your mental picture, the better. As you continue breathing and feeling grateful, go all out and truly design who you are going to be henceforth.

If your intention today is to be kind towards others, then *hear* yourself saying kind things to strangers for no reason. One smile or kind word can change someone's day. *See* the reaction in your kids, your friends, or your significant other when you tell them how much they matter to you.

Speak your gratitude out loud. For example, say: *"I am grateful that I am able to give those I love comfort, protection, stability, adventure, and enjoyment. I am grateful that I am kind and patient."* Acknowledge these attributes in the present tense. See and feel who you'd love, who you'd inspire, the difference you'd make in the world, and the qualities and principles by which you will live. Imagine every detail. Say, *"I am grateful that today I influenced someone's mood through my kindness. I am grateful to lead by example at work by being on time and productive. I model sincerity, loyalty, hard work, joy, perseverance, calmness, and compassion for others around me. I am grateful to be the change I want to see in the world."*

If your intention is to become a healthier person, fully restored from an illness, then see yourself enjoying the proper nutrition to help your body reach optimal vitality, exercise, love your body, and will it to heal.

Bring a mental picture into your heart of the person you desire to become. Forget about the person your parents told you ought to be, or what society has influenced you to want to be. Today is your chance to listen to your own heart and connect with your genuine self. Remember that connecting as many of your senses to the vision of the self you are creating living your life will help you with its manifestation. Picture how you want to behave as this new self today with your partner, your children, your pets, your friends. When you can match your actions to your intentions, your intentions to your emotions, and your emotions to your behavior, you will be connected to your future self.

Your life will always move in the direction of the words you say to yourself and the belief that you have about who you are and who you think yourself capable of becoming. So, when you give focused gratitude for the person you wish to become in the present moment, and you use the words *I am*, you are invoking divine energy, carrying enough power into the Universe to turn what you've proclaimed into reality. When you say, *"I am . . . that,"* you prophesize whatever it is that you place after your "I am" assertions.

Whether or not you are this person yet, don't worry. Believe (at least during your FMTG) that you already are. If you keep giving gratitude for your future self in the present tense, you will become whomever you intend yourself to be. The whole purpose here is to have you focus on all the positive things you would like to embody and move you away from thinking about the qualities you think you lack.

I find that we too often spend time focusing on the opposite of what we want. People worry too much about the things they don't want for their life and inadvertently, by giving thought and energy to that, it's what they attract. I hear people say, "I am never going to make it. I don't have what it takes. It is never going for happen to me," or "Winter is coming, and knowing my luck, I will get sick."

The sad reality is that the list is endless, and we are often unaware of the things we even tell ourselves and the power those thoughts and words carry. It is time for you to shift your focus away from the lack, away from the defeatist self-talk, and start creating in you the person you were meant to be. Remember, nothing is impossible. Nothing is far from your reach. If you can feel it in your heart and you can see the person you want to create in your mind—you will become that. Why? Because *you already are that person*. You could not conceive of everything you aspire to be and have unless it was already yours. It is in the Universe, in the Field, and it's up to you to act in accordance with the person of your dreams to materialize it.

I'd like to close this lesson with an inspiring testimonial from a student who has multiple sclerosis. He said, "Beyond grateful. My prayers have been answered for finding a daily prayer—and that is the prayer of gratitude! Today's FMTG was the most powerful meditation of my life. I was blissed out for over an hour with tears of joy streaming down my face envisioning who I wanted to become. So many things happened forty-eight hours after. I hiked through six inches of snow with my trekking polls for a little over a hundred yards, when three days ago, I could hardly walk ten yards with my walker on the sidewalk. Later I used my cane for walking, bouncing, and dancing around the bar, which I haven't been able to do in a very long time.

"Three years ago, I lost my ability to play the guitar and had lost the strength to project my voice and sign. Tonight, it was a different story. My rhythm and playing were just as good as I ever remembered them being, and my voice came back. My healing is in the present tense, and it is happening. I am so grateful to be part of this FMTG community."

When you can connect to the future self you want to create on a consistent basis, your brain and body will work in harmony to create the very state you are *feeling* through your creation.

When you feel you have completed your FMTG for today, close your exercise by expressing your gratitude, say, *"I am thankful to the Universe for the person I am and for the person that I am consciously choosing to become. I am blessed."*

DAY 4 REFLECTIONS

Use this space to write down any thoughts about your experience with gratitude on Day 4.

_____

_____

_____

_____

_____

_____

THE GRATITUDE BLUEPRINT

_____

_____

_____

_____

_____

_____

_____

_____

_____

_____

_____

_____

_____

_____

_____

_____

_____

_____

_____

_____

_____

_____

_____

_____

DAY 5

DESIGNING THE
BLUEPRINT OF YOUR LIFE

PURPOSE: *TO FOLLOW THE DIRECTIONS AND MAP TO
YOUR NEW LIFE.*

Welcome to Day 5! Wasn't yesterday amazing?! I hope you enjoyed visualizing the qualities you desire to embody and the person you want to become. Today we're going to go further, and have you begin designing the life that your new self will live.

Know that what you can dream of you can manifest and conceive. As unattainable and farfetched as the things may seem to be that come to your mind from now on, please don't judge them. Remember that in previous days you surrendered your judgments of things. You want to keep that up.

How does manifestation occur? We manifest anything we envision as present-occurring, but only to the degree that our subconscious mind believes it is possible to achieve and that we are worthy of deserving it. So, your job with your FMTG is to ensure your visions and desires are clear and that they are felt so intensely that new neural pathways grow, which reach deeply into the region of your medial brain. This ensures the images get imprinted into the subconscious mind. It is my personal opinion that the energy of your desired future literally encodes itself into the stem cells in your body. From there, I believe that it produces an energy signature that attracts a matching outcome from the quantum field.

You may have been manifesting all your life without realizing you were doing it or realizing the power within you. With FMTG, you are consciously participating in the process. As a Gratituder commented, "For me, this is about making the unconscious, conscious. I have patterns that have been on autopilot. I am taking back control of the flight. So grateful for this."

If you go into the Day 5 practice thinking and feeling that you are perhaps not good enough for your dreams, then what do you think you'll get? Something less. I know I've said this to you before, but it is worth repeating: The Universe gives to you only to the degree you feel you deserve the gift. Therefore, for the five minutes of your FMTG session this morning, forget whether or not you have the resources or the knowhow necessary to achieve your desire. The source of power you'll access doesn't care that, right now, you do or don't have the means or experience.

If, while you are dreaming and feeling your future, you get emotional, even better. I cannot tell you the number of tears of joy I've shed in seeing my life being created. Let yourself feel it. Be one with it. Step into that moment in time and give gratitude. Cry, smile, feel the love because that means it is feeling real to your body, and that is when you become the magnet for the miracles you like to see in your life. As a Gratituder of the online FMTG course said, "I never had plans for my future or expectations because my life was so tumultuous that I didn't have time to create, I was busy trying to overcome and handle all the challenges that life sent me. For the first time in thirty-five years, I am making plans for the future, and it feels great!"

If, while doing this exercise, any doubts arise, pay attention to them as well. The most important thing about this exercise is that you stay mindful of your deepest thoughts. If you are unable to connect to a future you would like to create, don't despair. This is a new exercise, and like anything new, it takes time and practice to overcome our body's resistance to things that feel foreign. Relax! Don't be hard on yourself if you don't get this on the first try. This is normal. Nobody is expecting you to get it perfect each time. I didn't! It took me a few tries, and I ended having to repeat this exercise sometimes in the mornings but also at the end of the day before bed. Little by little, I began to connect to the future I wanted. So, your job with FMTG is *not* to feel like you have to force things. Try it, if resistance surfaces/arises, be gentle with your thoughts. Do your best and know that you can always go back to this exercise and repeat—as the saying goes, Rome was not built in a day!

Empowerment coach Mary Morrissey offers a great analogy for the importance of homing in on what we want when we communicate with the Universe. She says it's like running an internet search. When we sit in front of our computers each day, all the information we possibly could search for is already available online, but what we get when we do a search is not all the information that is out there because we have to input a keyword or keyword phrase before we hit the enter button. Search engines only give us information that is similar to what we tell them we are interested in.[2]

I love this analogy! It is so true. The internet is equal to the Universe, where an infinite number of possibilities exists. Our thoughts and emotions are like a search engine. The Universe responds by providing what we claim and believe we deserve.

You are now going to focus all the energy you've freed after letting go of your past to creating a map to your future. You are designing the life you want to attract and manifest into physical reality. Begin to dream, think, and feel the things you want to attract in your life as if they have already happened and give gratitude for your desires even prior to having them. After that, surrender the need to set timelines. Surrender the need to control the outcome.

Create and feel your future life and then let go so that the Universe can go and do her job. The "how" is not up to you.

Take a step back in faith and watch the mysterious process of synchronicity unfold before your eyes.

When you feel and give gratitude for the things you desire as already attained, your body doesn't know the difference of an event that is happening by thought alone, to your body, you are living the event. Your body starts to produce the signature that matches the frequency of the Universe and in turn, she finds a way to mirror those vibrations back to you, and like magic, your life begins to unfold as the one you've experienced in the future, and your present mind collaborates to match those experiences.

Each time you say thank you ahead of the event, and you feel in your heart what it is like to already enjoy the life you are visualizing, a powerful vibration is created, and this is what bridges our outer and inner worlds. This is why it is important to train your mind and body to focus only on the things you desire. Sadly, we have been conditioned by our societal programming to focus more on the things we want to avoid in our lives. You may think that focusing on what you don't want will actually help you avoid them, but it is the opposite. You attract what you focus on.

Remember that in the realm of possibilities, all possibilities already exist, including the ones you like to avoid. To pull toward you a possibility you want, your thoughts must focus only on the one you desire. Then, by breathing gratitude into that thought—into its image in your mind—you give that possibility life to come into this world. The visualization of such a desired object is not enough to pull it from the Field. It must be accompanied by an emotion that is pure, and of such high-frequency energy that can make it pass your stem cell to reach the body.[1] and the only emotions that I personally know to be that powerful are gratitude and love. So, love the life you are creating. I don't know what it is you wish to manifest, but whatever it is, love it enough to birth it into life.

Are you ready to give this a try? Let's begin.

Close your eyes and place your hand over your heart. Breathe deeply and slowly and take a few moments to turn your attention inwards. Feel what it would be like to have the life you want right now. What things would you like to learn, do, and experience? Picture the things you wish to achieve, running vivid scenes of them in your mind like a movie—except that you are in it! Wow, can you see it now? Really get detailed and set no limits on your imagination.

Breathe and rejoice in what your mental movie is creating. Engage all your senses. Feel you are living that life right now. Make it real. Believe you are worthy of your desires.

What do you wish to create? A new job? A new home? A new relationship? Financial freedom? That trip you always wished to take, take it today. Remember, if you do a good job of visualizing and engaging all your senses, it will be as if you have really taken it. If it feels real, your brain will go to work to figure out the ways to match that blueprint you've given it. Feel what it feels like to already be on that vacation of your dreams. If your desire is to be somewhere to enjoy the beach, then hear the ocean waves and feel the sand on your feet. Taste that refreshing drink you are having, your hands get wet when you grab the glass that is full of condensation due to the contact of the ice against that hot tropical sun. Imagine the sensation of the contact of your first sip and how, as your taste buds taste that sweet cocktail, they thank you. *Mmm, yes!* It's wonderful, isn't it?

Say, *"I am grateful that I can be in this paradise and see the miracle of this ocean, the magnificent blue sky that looks like painted on a canvas with its perfect clouds. I am grateful to breathe this new air, taste the salty residue of the water on my skin. I am grateful to be seeing new places, new cultures, and people. I am grateful to feel the sunshine on my face, to enjoy the shade of green palm trees, and even enjoy this cold refreshing coconut water that nourishes my body."* Say whatever is true for you.

If your wish is to accomplish a great project, then see yourself achieving the end result. Witness in your mind and heart your sensation of pride, the satisfaction in your heart because your long hours and sacrifice have paid off.

That home that you have always dreamed of having, see it in your mind. See yourself signing the contract to purchase it, and for the exact amount that you wish to pay for it. Feel your pride when you tell your family you are moving. That backyard you wish for your kids? See them running in it, maybe big enough to have a trampoline for them to jump on, a pool? The beautiful deck? See yourself and your loved one having a nice glass of wine while you sit and watch the sunset from it. See your significant other rejoicing as you decorate every room and put little touches here and there that make a house into a home. What is the street where you want to live? Do you see yourself driving towards your new home after a day's work? What color is the house? Design all the rooms you wish to have. That closet you always dreamed of having, it can be yours today! You are the architect, remember?

Say, *"I am grateful to have a blessed and wonderful life, free of financial stress, in a home that is harmonious and peaceful. I am grateful to enjoy the fruits of my labor with people I adore. I am grateful that life gifts me more opportunities for celebration than sad ones. Grateful for the friends and family I can count on for support."*

If it is health you are desiring, then see yourself optimally well and spontaneously healed of any condition that has been troubling you. Feel in your body what would it be like to have your functioning fully restored and breathe gratitude into body parts that were involved in any issue. See yourself enjoying all the things that you may not have been able to enjoy due to an illness.

Still, with your eyes closed and hand on your heart, picture an event, and see it through in its totality. If you were fully healed, what would you be able to wear? What would you be able to eat? How does it taste? What would you be able to do? Whatever it is that limits you due to your illness, see yourself enjoying life. Feel your body in perfect health. And say, *"I am grateful that my good health enables me to play the sports that I love. I am grateful for having the energy levels that enable me to run after my kids (grandkids, pet)."* Say whatever is true for you and see it in your mind.

When you are finished with your FMTG for today, end your session by expressing your gratitude in advance. As an example, you can end with, *"I am thankful to the Universe for empowering me to manifest the life of my dreams. Thank you."*

DAY 5 REFLECTIONS

Use this space to write down any thoughts about your experience with gratitude on Day 5.

_____

_____

_____

_____

_____

_____

_____

_____

_____

_____

_____

_____

_____

_____

_____

_____

_____

_____

_____

_____

DAY 6

CREATING THE INTIMATE RELATIONSHIP OF YOUR DREAMS

PURPOSE: *TO MANIFEST THE RIGHT PERSON TO SHARE YOUR LIFE.*

It doesn't matter if you are married or single; you deserve an ideal relationship. Designing a blueprint for love is one of the most important parts of anyone's life. One of the main reasons we incarnate is to experience love in the physical form. But of course, many of us are not strangers to hurt and disappointment in our romantic relationships. That is why there is the saying "Love hurts"! The reality, however, is that genuine love doesn't hurt. Love is pure and unchangeable. It is the behavior of people that hurts us. It is unrequited love that hurts. It is loss that hurts. Once I understood this, I stopped blocking myself from expressing love and allowing love into my life.

Consciously, I have always been a romantic at heart. I loved the idea of love! Subconsciously, I was petrified of love because I believed that love was the root of my pain. Given that we attract experiences that match the ideas we've programmed into our subconscious minds, how was I going to find a life partner with a belief like that? It did not matter how much I thought I wanted romantic love in my life. That was on the surface. My underlying beliefs were blocking love from coming to me. And I was not even aware that I was doing so. As a result of my subconscious limiting beliefs, I ended several relationships that could have been great, including my marriage.

Some of the subconscious thoughts I had were, *"Relationships don't last. Sooner or later, people leave. I will be abandoned. It is not safe to give your heart. I have to protect my heart by building walls."* Do any of these thoughts sound familiar?

Before you begin your FMTG session, Day 6, reflect on what your deepest thoughts about love are. Bring awareness to what you truly believe because these ideas could be what has been blocking your ability to attract love or stop you from giving and receiving love openly with your committed partner. You must be honest because, if you have been blocking yourself subconsciously, you will need to prune those beliefs and replace them with better ones that are more in alignment with the reality you wish to create before you can manifest it. Not every relationship is doomed to end badly, so if you play your cards right and learn to love your partner from a place of pure gratitude, you can grow old together and stay in love.

Whether or not you are in a romantic relationship, I invite you to design the romance of your dreams. If you are in a relationship, use this FMTG session to express gratitude for what is working well for you and then to envision how you and your partner can improve it. Throughout a lifetime, it is possible to fall in love multiple times with the same person as both of you grow and evolve as people. Today, you will do your best to envision all the ways in which you can become a better husband, wife, girlfriend, and partner. Make the intention to be perhaps more expressive, more helpful, less reactive, more loving, romantic, spontaneous.

If you are not currently in a relationship, your job right now is to use your FMTG to design the blueprint of the relationship you would like, down to naming the qualities of the partner you would like to attract into your life. Are they compassionate, generous, a good listener, resourceful, financially stable, physically fit, loving, or kind? Say whatever you would like to manifest. It is a lot to do in five minutes, I know. Stay longer in your meditation if you wish or come back to this visualization at any point. Let images rise to the surface and immerse yourself in gratitude for them.

Don't worry about not having a partner or that your partner disappoints you right now. You must say these things as if you already do have a partner who matches this vision. Be precise with your language, so that nothing is left up to interpretation. The Universe is literal, remember? If your intention is to marry, then say that. If your intention is to have companionship, then state that. Be as clear as you can in describing what you want to attract or bring out in your current partner.

When I did my FMTG, I declared my desire to attract a partner that was fully evolved and complete with a whole life for himself. The Universe literally sent me someone too self-sufficient for my liking. He has a complete life of his own. In the beginning, this reality was difficult for me. I was not used to someone not needing me to save him. I attracted someone who is fulfilled by his work, the service he does for his community, full of love, and extremely busy with his beautiful children. The man is so busy that I don't spend long periods of time with him. What I really thought I would get when I said, "Someone who was self-sufficient and complete" was someone who was financially free and would have more time to be with me. But what the Universe heard is what I asked for—exactly. I was gifted with a partner that prevents me from becoming codependent.

I hope you see how important it is to be precise and clear about what you truly are creating. To attract a person that loves you, honors you, provides adventure, laugher, intimacy, and loyalty, you must first live by these values yourself. That is why you worked on designing the person you want to become on Day 4 this week. We cannot attract things that we aren't ourselves. As I've said multiple times, the Universe is a mirror. Thus, you will attract partnerships that reflect your deepest subconscious beliefs and programs.

As you learned in Week Three, if you ignore the parts of yourself that need healing, you will continue to attract partners that shine a light on those areas. Do you want that? Probably not.

Really, what you want is to attract your equal, someone who can stand beside the newly empowered you and walk with you through this miraculous thing called life. So, if you desire to attract someone who is stable, *be* stable! Do you want to be with someone who is great at intimacy? Then *be* willing to be vulnerable and open. Do you want to attract someone who is a great communicator who is expressive and loving? Then *be* those things yourself.

Focus on creating and being the best version of yourself so that you can attract the best version of someone else. We can teach people how to treat us. The more you can be yourself—authentic, vulnerable, and uncompromising of your values—the better chance you will have of attracting a great love into your life. If you embody high-frequency energy, such as love, compassion, gratitude, authenticity, and forgiveness, you will raise your chances of attracting all the great things that are also vibrating at those high levels of frequency.

Ready to create an ideal relationship? Let's do it!

With your eyes closed and hand over your heart, begin to breathe slowly and deeply. Bring to your heart the image of the person you love or wish to attract. Breathe appreciation for that relationship into your heart as you imagine some of the things you would like to experience with this individual.

Whatever it is that you want to experience, visualize it as happening in real-time. See yourself already enjoying doing those things with your loved one and try to experience these scenes with all of your senses. What do you hear, see, smell, taste, touch? Where are you? Who is with you? What is happening? How do you feel?

Breathe gratitude as you see yourself walking hand in hand with your loved one, enjoying the simple things in life, having a cup of coffee together, playing a card game, sitting while you read a book, cuddling by a fire. Can you feel it? Say, *"I am grateful that I am blessed with a partner with whom I love waking up. I will not let this day end without demonstrating it to my loved one."*

Each time you feel your heart beating on the palm of your hand, breathe in gratitude for having this wonderful love in your life. Feel your heart expand with love as you say words like, *"I am grateful for having such a loving relationship. I have a partner who honors and respects me. I have a partner with whom I look forward to growing old. I am grateful that I have healthy boundaries. I am grateful to have a partner who is self-sufficient, fully evolved, and complete. I am grateful that we share values and preferences. I am grateful that we have fantastic sex. I am grateful that we are the ideal companions. I am grateful that we make each other laugh and trust each other completely. I am grateful that I am my best self, and like myself, when I am around this person. I am grateful that we can rely on one another."*

Imagine what it feels like to already be in this amazing relationship. Can you see it? Can you feel it? Focus on the outcome, not how you arrived at it. Do not worry about the *how*, as it is not up to you. Immerse yourself in gratitude for this beautiful gift from the Universe.

And when you feel you have completed your FMTG session for today, end it by expressing your gratitude in advance by saying something like, *"I am thankful to the Universe for the relationship that is already on its way to me."* If you are in a relationship, end your practice by saying, *"I am thankful to the Universe for transforming and improving my relationship, for I now enjoy the kind of partner and love I deserve."*

Focus on the feeling of already being with the person of your dreams. Trust me, that person is out there waiting for you. As much as you are seeking the ideal partner, the ideal partner is also seeking you! If you are in a current relationship, be present, and be relentless in pursuing your desires as you witness your intimate relationship flourish and blossom.

DAY 6 REFLECTIONS

Use this space to write down any thoughts about your experience with gratitude on Day 6.

_____

_____

_____

_____

_____

_____

WALEUSKA LAZO

DAY 7

WRITING A LIFE INTENTION STATEMENT (EULOGY)

PURPOSE: *TO ENVISION THE LEGACY BY WHICH YOU WISH TO BE REMEMBERED.*

Wow, can you believe we have made it to the end? It has been an amazing journey of learning, reflecting, and creating. Today, you will pull together all you've learned about the person you want to be and the life you want to lead and draft a life intention statement. Writing a life intention statement is the same as writing a eulogy, with one important difference: You are alive.

This FMTG exercise is important because now that you know the qualities of the person you want to be and the life you want to manifest, you are able to create a farewell tribute to honor the memory of the contributions you will have made throughout your lifespan. Isn't this amazing? After you immerse yourself in gratitude for five minutes today, you are going to actually take part in writing the final speech describing the legacy you would like to leave behind and be remembered by once you are no longer on this plane of existence.

How many people would you guess do this type of exercise? Not enough.

Have you ever wondered if the spirits of departed people, now in a casket, can hear what others say about them? I have. I was recently at the funeral of someone I did not know personally, the sister-in-law of a good friend of mine who is like family to me. I attended to show my solidarity and respect for his family's loss. Best decision. It was the most beautiful, heartfelt eulogy I have ever heard a son and daughter give to their mother. Although I did not have the honor of meeting this human being, I walked away feeling privileged to have met her through the stories her children told. I left with a renewed sense of inspiration for living and a sense of the legacy I would like to leave behind when I die. At that moment, I understood what I wanted my children to say about me, their mother, when I was gone—and in order to accomplish that, I knew I would have to embody, while alive, all the qualities I want my beloved daughters to mention.

Have you thought about the legacy you want to leave behind for others to honor? What would you like to hear your loved ones say about the life you've lived? What is the story they can tell? The life intention statement you're going to create today should contain the essence of your ideal life as you want it remembered. Describe significant milestones, events, and accomplishments, people you loved and touched, and the impact your presence made on those who knew you and the world.

Since you are writing your life intention statement while you are still alive, your FMTG session today gives you a chance to dream about it.

Today is the last day of the program. Your mission going forward is to use your FMTG tools every day to connect to your life vision.

What really matters in life is not the dates on your tombstone but the dash between those numbers, which represents how well you lived and how much you loved.

How do you wish your dash to sum up your existence?

With your eyes closed and your hand over your heart, breathe life into your beautiful lungs and connect to the inevitable day when you will no longer be here. Don't be scared. There is nothing to fear in doing this exercise. In fact, doing this will leave you feeling fully alive because, as you probably experienced in Week Two, when you connected to your mortality, this exercise reminds you that each day is a gift. This perspective makes our lives more meaningful. In my opinion, the prospect of death is what makes life as precious as it is.

Lying in your bed, imagine your funeral. See your loved ones expressing their last farewells to you and bring this image to your heart. As you do, say, *"I am grateful that while I am alive, I can act as I want my loved ones to remember me. I am* grateful that I can use each day to embody the qualities and values that are reflected in my intention statement. I am also grateful that I can do deeds that will make a mark that matters. It is not how much money or how many things I accumulate that count. It is the hearts I touch, the lives I improve, the example I set, the joy I choose to express, the fears I overcome, the hugs I give, the friendships I make, the love I cultivate, the adventures I go on, the places I visit, the kindnesses I offer, the words of advice I bestow, the arguments I settle, the anger I heal, the people I forgive, and the gifts I express. These things are, from this day forward, my legacy."

Imagine looking at your dead body and loving yourself. Send gratitude back for the entire life you have lived at every step of the way and in its entirety. Immerse yourself in gratitude for your soul for allowing you to have this learning opportunity and doing the best you could with it.

When you feel you have completed your FMTG session, close it out by saying something like, *"I am thankful to the Universe in advance for the life I have led."*

THERE IS SOMETHING incredibly humbling and empowering that takes place inside of us when we see our lives flash before us while doing this visualization. After you have completed your FMTG gratitude immersion, please turn the page and write down what you imagined.

DAY 7 REFLECTIONS

Today's writing exercise is different. You are at the end of the FMTG experience, and you have sent gratitude to your dying self, looking back at your entire lifetime. On this page, write down your life intention statement or eulogy. Afterward, you can live into the meaning of these words.

Use this space to outline your eulogy. One way you could do this is to start with a short biographical overview of where and when you were born, memories from childhood, and the names of your family members. Describe significant family events and the date and place of your passing (assume for now this will occur where you live). Write any special, significant stories you want the people present at your memorial service to know, special qualities and skills you possess and your achievements, things you were known for doing. End your statement with words of comfort, pearls of wisdom, and a final goodbye.

I also invite you to write down one special word or a short phrase or a quote that encapsulates the essence of who you are. Perhaps this is a phrase depicting what you stood for that could be used as an epitaph engraved on your tombstone. What would that be? Take your time to think of this. Reflect on it.

Dr. Seuss (Theodore Geisel) chose the epitaph "Don't cry because it's over. Smile because it happened." Another nice one I've seen is: "To live in the hearts of those we love is never to die." The one I came up with for myself is: "Here lies a grateful heart."

The point of this writing exercise is to ground you so that you can begin to be everything that you want to see reflected in the hearts and minds of your loved ones and colleagues and on your memorial stone.

After doing this writing exercise, one of my Gratituders reflected, "I had never allowed myself to think of the things I would like others to say at my funeral because I thought it was a bit egotistical of me to assume that others would view me in such high regard. Now I see how doing this can help shape my actual path in life. I want to be all the things I wish people to love and remember me for. So, I will not fear this exercise anymore. My legacy matters."

Here is an example you can use as a guide. "A dearly beloved and devoted son, husband, father, grandfather, brother, uncle, and special friend. A noble, kind, and gentle man, loved by all who knew him, who labored all his life so his family could enjoy. Peoples' lives are enriched by your goodness. You are forever remembered, loved, and in our hearts. Your presence we miss, your legacy we treasure. Your strength and courage illuminate, guide, and inspire us. To the world, you are great; to us, you are the world. We love you always, now and forever."

Your personal life intention statement should be a celebration of your life, of the person others will have come to know you as. In writing it, assume you have made your life count! Let this statement teach and inspire you. Read it often. Connect to it. Walk your talk. Be all that you want to be. Only you can design your life because you are the architect. Remember? So, go on and design a great life. I know you can!

Life Intention Statement (Eulogy)

_____

_____

_____

_____

_____

_____

_____

_____

_____

_____

_____

_____

_____

_____

_____

_____

_____

_____

_____

_____

_____

_____

_____

_____

_____

_____

_____

_____

_____

_____

_____

_____

_____

_____

_____

_____

_____

_____

_____

_____

_____

_____

_____

_____

_____

_____

THE GRATITUDE BLUEPRINT

_____

_____

_____

_____

_____

_____

_____

_____

_____

_____

_____

_____

_____

_____

_____

_____

_____

_____

_____

_____

_____

_____

_____

_____

_____

_____

_____

_____

_____

AFTERWORD

*THE ACT OF EXPRESSING
GRATITUDE IN ADVANCE IGNITES
THE FREQUENCY TO ATTRACT
MIRACLES.*

Writing this book for you has been a pure delight. Through the process of testing the Five Minutes to Gratitude system, I met many wonderful people from around the globe. I was speechless when I saw how FMTG transformed their lives. I am grateful that I have now been able to spread the practice further and wider and to have welcomed you into my community of Gratituders. I hope the experience of reading the book and experimenting with this practice and its underlying concepts has been as meaningful for you as it was for the participants in my early research groups.

Over the course of the last twenty-eight days, you have done an incredible amount of work. You can be proud of the effort, discipline, commitment, and bravery you have demonstrated, which has enabled you to reprogram your mind and break free of limiting subconscious patterns and emotional blocks. By now, you have had the experience of living as an empowered, grateful self, and it is my hope that you will choose to continue using the FMTG practice regularly to uplift your mind and mood.

FMTG is now as much yours as it is mine. FMTG is your tool to use daily, and hopefully, for the rest of your life. Your needs and desires may change from time to time, as you face future challenges. Continue using your feeling-based FMTG practice to cocreate with the Universe. Make use of your FMTG as often as you need. Remember, you can now communicate directly with the Universe in a language that she understands.

My dear Gratituder, as you go on with your life beyond the time we've spent together, it's my honor to share a few additional pearls of wisdom with you.

You and you alone can manifest the life of your dreams through cocreation with the Universe—not your circumstances, not the people around you—only you have that power. While nobody is a "magician" that can make things happen miraculously on the spot, we can welcome the power of cocreation by staying in the frequency of gratitude as much as possible. Never forget that if you are clear about what you want to create and who you want to be, declare your intention to the Universe, focus on the outcome as already having it, and say thank you *in advance* for your gifts and blessings, then the things you desire will find you, and you will be who you want to be with ease. We always attract things that are on the same frequency as us.

Protect your dreams at all costs. Do not listen to those giving you a hundred reasons why your dreams cannot come true. People mean well, but often speak to us from a place of fear. You must be relentless in safeguarding the quality of your energy field. Be careful about the ideas you allow to take residence in your mind. As soon as someone starts to give you advice that is not in alignment with what you are consistently creating, stop them. Be kind, but firm.

Ignore and block anything negative that goes against what you are trying to accomplish. What may seem impossible to those who are looking at you is not impossible to the Universe. People don't know what you know or what you are doing with your FMTG rituals! Through FMTG, you are conspiring with a force that defies the conditions of our physical world. In "reality," you are conspiring with the force that created everything. Anything is possible.

The Universe responds to your *strongest* feeling every day. If you find yourself feeling fearful or doubtful, you may negate the wonderful work you have done in visualizing optimal health, great achievements, close, supportive relationships, and other details of the life you want to create. FMTG helps ensure your strongest feeling of the day is an elevated feeling. Staying in the frequency of your creations will require you to be vigilant, not just about ignoring what other people say, but also, and more importantly, regarding the quality of your own thoughts, emotions, and actions.

Dwell in gratefulness. Just as you have learned to begin the day giving thanks, always close your day by giving thanks in advance for anything in your life.

Rejoice with love and gratitude at the knowledge that you are not alone. There is a great ally at your disposal: The Universe. Feel grateful that a divine force is constantly cocreating with you and be appreciative. Invoking the feeling of gratitude in your body that your outcome is present and real for you is a signal to the Universe that what you desire has already happened. And so, the Universe mirrors it and sends you more of the same. It is beautiful to watch this process in action!

Be grateful for every breath of air that you inhale. That's life you are breathing. Today and every day, remember that this moment is the only moment you have and say thank you for your life. Gratitude is only your next breath away.

When we are grateful, even in the face of our difficulties, we are less fearful and more resilient. Remember this as you are creating your future. Upon occasion, you will be confronted with challenges and detours. Your spirit may even be tested to the point where you come to wonder if all the things you have learned and practiced in this process are real and possible. Stay the course.

The last piece of wisdom I leave with you is to trust the Universe. Don't try to control outcomes or force the world to conform to how you think it should be. Those are paths to frustration. Just trust the Universe. She knows what she is doing. If your dreams are taking longer than you expected to manifest, drop your expectations.

If you are too rigid about the appearance and timing of your creations, you may miss seeing other opportunities that the Universe is putting in your way. Remember, although you've now created the blueprint for the life you want and who you want to be, there is still a lot to discover. I firmly believe that when we can feel gratitude and acceptance in our hearts for what is being presented to us at any moment, we open ourselves to wonderful possibilities that we didn't know existed.

I saw a beautiful passage on the wall of a temple I visited in Capernaum, a town by the Sea of Galilee where Jesus preached, that read: "The Universe answers prayers in three ways. 'Yes' —because you deserve it. 'No' —because you deserve better. And 'Not Yet' —because the best is yet to come."

Sometimes we plan the life we wish to have and get surprised by the Universe with something even better. Sometimes we don't dream big enough. Thankfully, the Universe loves us too much to allow us to settle for second best.

Thank you for the opportunity to guide you through the FMTG journey. I hope it has been an incredible one for you. I wish you success in your endeavors, peace in your heart, love in your home, and enough gratitude to last you a lifetime.

APPENDIX

TWENTY-EIGHT DAYS OF GRATITUDE AT A GLANCE

Week One Gratitude Topics

Day 1. Gratitude

Day 2. Your Immediate Surroundings

Day 3. Nature and Our Planet

Day 4. Your Work and Workplace

Day 5. Your Children and Other Tender Beings

Day 6. Your Significant Others (Present or Past)

Day 7. Your Parents

Week Two Gratitude Topics

Day 1. Your Character-Defining Moments

Day 2. The Little Things Your Partner Does

Day 3. Your Friends and Colleagues

Day 4. Self-Love and Appreciation

Day 5. Your Closed Doors

Day 6. Your Body's Invisible Activities

Day 7. Your Mortality

Week Three Gratitude Topics

Day 1. Healing Your Past

Day 2. Healing Your Inner Child

Day 3. Healing Your Intimate Relationships

Day 4. Forgiving Others

Day 5. Forgiving Yourself

Day 6. Healing Your Limiting Beliefs

Day 7. Healing Your Illnesses

Week Four Gratitude Topics

Day 1. Surrendering Judgment

Day 2. Finding the Gift in Your Emotional Pain

Day 3. Your Core Moments

Day 4. Becoming the Person of Your Dreams

Day 5. Designing the Blueprint of Your Life

Day 6. Creating the Intimate Relationship of Your Dreams

Day 7. Writing a Life Intention Statement (Eulogy)

ACKNOWLEDGMENTS

I am grateful to the Gratituders who were the first to accept my invitation to join me to test the concepts and principles described in this book. They are the pioneers of what is now known as the FMTG, Gratitude Experiment Course! Thank you for trusting me with your fears and aspirations. Thank you for bravely opening up and sharing without judgment. Thank you for your compassion, feedback, and support.

Helen Ackley
Lena Artinian
Shelly Ashford
Glenda Barber
Joan Mary Belford
Heidi Benson
Jane Bowhay-Clarke
Thasveer Brar
Julie Lynn Corbett
Kim Doherty
Jason Dovin
Elizabeth Meghan Dwyer
Dana Ecelberger
Lorraine Farrugia
Lara Marie Ford
Ali Gilling

Susana Gozalo
Alycia Green
Sigrídur Hrund Guomunddsdottir
Maree Verdon Hendrickx
Liana Kaiser
Silvi Lion
Joanne Malone
Barry White McCarthy
Safiyyah U. Mohammed
Gilda Morales
Deva Neely
Susana Rantala Nelson
Roxana Nica
Emily Nousbaum
Courtney Parkinson
Edith Rico
Bailey Ann Stout
Jackie Walton
François Wognum

I am also deeply indebted to and grateful for the contributions of François Wognum, who has so generously given his time and technical expertise to make the Gratitude Experiment course user-friendly and accessible for all Gratituders.

Special thanks to the FMTG Team, Terry Turriff Bergdoll, Jenny Smith, Nish Takia, Julie Kessler, Maureen Pankhurst Schlachter, Susana Gozalo, and Swati Taneja, for believing in FMTG and being lights for this work in the world.

Barry McCarthy, for being my biggest cheerleader and always having my back.

Elizabeth Meghan Dwyer, for her tireless love and support of FMTG and helping me carry the torch of such a powerful and life transformative system.

Special thanks to my beautiful partner, Michael Kalles, who has been there for me every step of this incredible journey, proudly encouraging me to continue the work of transforming lives.

To my children, Victoria and Emma Feldberg, who are the engine that propels my every dream, thank you for encouraging me to do this work and for always reminding me of the difference I am making in the world.

To my developmental editor, Stephanie Gunning, who assisted me in making the dream of this book come true from start to finish, and who was the one suggested that I should put a gratitude course on Facebook to test the exercises in my manuscript. Without her encouragement, I would never have taken the leap. I will be forever grateful to her for believing in my vision. Thanks also to the Gunning Writer Works team: Gus Yoo, for his cover design, and Najat Washington, for her assistance with the interior layout.

Last but not least, to my business partner, Jeffrey Feldberg, who is my guiding light. Thank you! Without your encouragement and vision, *The Gratitude Blueprint* would not exist. It was your love, vision, consistent guidance, help, and support that gave me the strength and drive to make my magnum opus a reality.

NOTES

Introduction

1. Paul Nussbaum. "Get to Know Your Brain," Dr. Nussbaum's Brain Health Lifestyle (accessed December 14, 2019), http://www.paulnussbaum.com/gettoknow.html.
2. Ibid.

Week One Introduction

1. Robert F. Furchgott," Wikipedia.com (accessed April 9, 2020).
2. "Ralph Waldo Emerson Quotes," BrainyQuote.com (accessed December 14, 2019).

Week One, Day 3. Nature and Our Planet

1. Lynn Carter. "How Many Meteorites Hit Earth Each Year? (Intermediate)" Ask an Astronomer (accessed December 14, 2019), http://curious.astro.cornell.edu/about-us/75-our-solar-system/comets-meteors-and-asteroids/meteorites/313-how-many-meteorites-hit-earth-each-year-intermediate.

Week One, Day 4. Your Work and Workplace

1. Wayne Dyer. "Dr. Wayne Dyer: Living the Wisdom of the Tao," DrWayneDyer.com (accessed December 2019).

Week Two Introduction

1. "EMF—Electromagnetic Frequency," *E-motion Health Interviews*, season 1, episode 7 (2014), Gaia.com.
2. *Resonance: Beings of Frequency*, written and directed by James Russell (January 1, 2013).
3. Clarity Coaching. "This New Science Will Blow Your Mind. Dr. Bruce Lipton Shocked the World with His Discovery," YouTube (May 15, 2019).
4. Law of Attraction Coaching. "Bruce Lipton: Learn How to Control Your Mind," YouTube (August 19, 2019).
5. "Map of Spirituality," Master Mindo (accessed February 20, 2020), http://www.mapofspirituality.org/map-of-spirituality.
6. Molly Lannon Kenny. "The Winds of God's Grace Are Always Blowing, It Is for us to Raise Our Sails," MollyLannonKenny.org blog (February 14, 2018).
7. Gregg Braden. "Human by Design: Day 2, Session 1," season 1, episode 3 (June 2019), Gaia.com.
8. Gregg Braden. "Missing Links: Awakening the Heart-Brain Union," season 1 episode 11 (March 9, 2017), Gaia.com.
9. Gregg Braden. *Secrets of the Lost Mode of Prayer: The Hidden Power of Beauty, Blessing, Wisdom, and Hurt* (Carlsbad, CA.: Hay House, 2006).

Week Two, Day 3. Your Friends and Colleagues

1. "Dr. Brené Brown: The Anatomy of Trust," Oprah's SuperSoul Conversations (April 15, 2019).

Week Two, Day 6. Your Body's Invisible Activities

1. Diane Wells. "Facts about the Heart You Didn't Know," Healthline (July 6, 2017), https://www.healthline.com/health/fun-facts-about-the-heart.
2. Tobey Jordan. "101 Amazing Eye Facts," Lenstore.com.uk (June 27, 2019).

Week Three Introduction

1. Gregg Braden. *Secrets of the Lost Mode of Prayer: The Hidden Power of Beauty, Blessing, Wisdom, and Hurt* (Carlsbad, CA.: Hay House, 2006).
2. "Larry Dossey on the Healing Power of Prayer," *Inspirations with Lisa Garr*, season 1, episode, 16, Gaia.com (2012).
3. "Awakening the Heart-Brain Union," *Missing Links with Gregg Braden*, season 1 episode 11, Gaia.com (March 9, 2017).
4. "You Are the Placebo with Joe Dispenza," *Inspirations with Lisa Garr*, season 6, episode 16, Gaia.com (June 2014).

Week Three, Day 1: Healing Your Past

1. Lisa Mack. "Trauma, Body Memories, and How to Heal Them," The Body Is Not an Apology (April 9, 2019), https://thebodyisnotanapology.com/magazine/what-are-body-memories-and-how-to-heal-them.

Week Three, Day 3. Healing Your Intimate Relationships

1. "Marianne Williamson: The Spiritual Purpose of Relationships," *Oprah's SuperSoul Conversations* (May 8, 2019).

Week Three, Day 4. Forgiving Others

1. John MacArthur. "Unmasking the Betrayer. John 13:17–30," Grace to You (accessed February 20, 2020), https://www.gty.org/library/articles/P26/unmasking-the-betrayer.

Week Three, Day 7. Healing Your Illnesses

1. "Intuitive Healing with Inna Segal" *Inspirations with Lisa Garr*, season 4, episode, 26, Gaia.com (October 10, 2013).
2. Link Media. "We control Our Genes—Bruce Lipton," YouTube (September 16, 2016), https://youtu.be/i67g6_w2c2Y.

Week Four, Day 1. Surrendering Judgment

1. Ecclesiastes. 3:1.
2. "How Suffering Transforms Us with Rabbi Steve Leder," *Inspirations with Lisa Garr*, season 10, episode 12, Gaia.com (May 20, 2019).

Week Four, Day 2. Finding the Gift in Your Emotional Pain

1. *Finding Joe*, written and directed by *Patrick Takaya Solomon* (2011).
2. "How Suffering Transforms Us with Rabbi Steve Leder," *Inspirations with Lisa Garr*, season 10, episode 12 (May 20, 2019), Gaia.com.
3. Oprah Winfrey. "Dr. Edith Eva Eger: The Choice," *Supersoul Sunday*, season 9, episode 908 (June 16, 2019).

Week Four, Day 4. Becoming the Person of Your Dreams

1. Ed Mylett. "Unlock the Unlimited Power of Your Mind Today! Ed Mylett and Dr. Joe Dispenza," YouTube.com (March 29, 2019), https://youtu.be/ereahWKwNV8.
2. "Creating the Life of Your Dreams with Mary Morrissey," *Inspirations with Lisa Garr*, season 5, episode 9 (December 2013), Gaia.com (December 2013).

Week Four, Day 5. Designing the Blueprint of Your Life

1. Lisa Garr. "The Aware Show's NeuroSummit III: Dr. Joe Dispenza Interviewed by Lisa Garr," YouTube (February 3, 2015), https://youtu.be/BW6a2t5myIA.

RESOURCES

After doing FMTG for twenty-eight days, you are well on your way to establishing a permanent attitude of gratitude. I encourage you to continue your daily immersion in this powerful process. You may go back to the beginning of the book and start over or dive deeper into specific topics. For additional resources, please visit my website and take one of my workshops and subscribe to my blog.

www.WaleuskaLazo.com

FREE BOOK GIFTS

I'd like to gift you with a free download of an audio chapter from my book *The Best Worst Thing That Happened to Me*. Pick that up at: https://www.waleuskalazo.com/freechapter and a free guided audio gratitude meditation, which you can get at https://waleuskalazo.com/bookgift

CONNECT WITH ME ON THE SOCIAL NETWORKS

Facebook.com/waleuska.lazo

Twitter.com/WaleuskaLazo

Instagram.com/waleuskalazo

Linkedin.com/in/waleuska-lazo-337623141

https://www.youtube.com/c/WaleuskaLazo

FACEBOOK GRATITUDE COMMUNITY

Your purchase of this book makes you eligible to join the Gratitude Community Facebook group. The benefits of belonging are that you will be among FMTG alumni and current students, making this a wonderfully supportive environment where you can ask questions and participate in healing activities that run throughout the year. It is also the place where I test new material. Join at: https://www.facebook.com/groups/760695044743534

TAKE A FACILITATED FMTG COURSE WITH ME

Join an interactive and facilitated FMTG course. Check for dates at: https://fmtg.us

INVITE ME TO SPEAK TO YOUR READING CLUB OR HEALING CIRCLE

I do workshops live over Zoom as well as in person. At these events, I teach people the importance of self-care and gratitude and how to gain perspective on their lives. A big part of this for participants involves learning how to shift the way they think and feel about painful events and change the energy they have attached to those events so they can heal their lives. If you believe this is of interest to your group or organization, contact me by email at waleuska@fmtg.us

ABOUT THE AUTHOR

Photo by Giulia Ciampini

WALEUSKA LAZO, creator of the twenty-eight-day online course FMTG, the Gratitude Experiment, is a passionate, expressive serial entrepreneur and divorced mother of two. Born in Nicaragua, Waleuska immigrated to Canada with her family as a teen. She earned a bachelor of arts degree and a master's degree in criminal justice from the University of Toronto. Currently, she splits her time between homes in Hollywood, Florida, in the United States, and Toronto, Ontario, in Canada.

In 1995, Waleuska cofounded Embanet™, a pioneering e-learning provider of higher education solutions and services, with her former husband and another business partner. They sold the company to Pearson in 2007. In 2009, she cofounded the Magnum Opus Development Group, a real estate firm that builds homes for discerning home buyers. In 2011, Waleuska founded DreamCatcher Print, a book publishing venture through which she has published a series of books about real-life heroes for young readers and books on personal transformation for adult readers. Works include *The Gift of Bravery: The Story of Eli Cohen* (2019), *Confessions from a Mom to Her Child* (2019), and her memoir, *The Best Worst Thing that Happened to Me* (2018). Waleuska attributes her successes to leading a life focused on service.

A SMALL REQUEST

Thank you for reading *The Gratitude Blueprint*. I am positive if you follow what I've written, you will be on the way to the creation of your ideal life and extraordinary happiness.

I have a small, quick favor to ask. Would you mind taking a minute or two and leaving an honest review of this book on Amazon? Reviews are the very best way to spread word of this book so others may purchase it and benefit from the technique it teaches; and I read all the customer reviews I get, looking for helpful feedback.

If you have any questions, want to share an FMTG story with me, or would like to tell me what you think about *The Gratitude Blueprint*, I can be reached by email at waleuska@fmtg.us. I'd love to hear from you!

Lightning Source UK Ltd.
Milton Keynes UK
UKHW021833260722
406402UK00009B/2135